Rathgar

A HISTORY

Rathgar

A HISTORY

MAURICE CURTIS

The
History
Press
Ireland

First published 2015

The History Press Ireland
50 City Quay
Dublin 2
Ireland
www.thehistorypress.ie

British Library Cataloguing in Publication Data.
A catalogue record for this book is available from the British Library.

ISBN 978 1 84588 886 2

Typesetting and origination by The History Press

CONTENTS

Acknowledgements   6

Introduction   8

1. Early History, the Castle and the Cusack Family   11
2. Pleasant Houses and Detached Villas, 1750–1850   16
3. Rathgar and the Township, 1847–1862   23
4. Trams and Transport – The Vulture of Dartry Hall   30
5. Thank Heavens for Rathgar – The Exclusivity of the 1930s   39
6. Steeples, Spires, Servants and Synagogues   43
7. The High Field – Different Houses for Different Eras   54
8. Rathgar Avenue, Garville and the Greek Revival   63
9. Rathgar Road and Villadom   82
10. The Windmill and the Washerwoman – Orwell   103
11. Dartry Road and the Steamboat Ladies   122
12. Zion, Bewley's and Bushy   130
13. Grosvenor, Kenilworth and the Gothic   138
14. James Joyce's Old Triangle   148
15. Sport and Music   154
16. Rathgar Village – Shops and Businesses   159

Bibliography   167

Notes   169

ACKNOWLEDGEMENTS

Many people in Rathgar were of immense help in writing this book. Among those I must include, Anthony Goulding, Eileen Clancy, Revd Stephen Farrell, Ged Walsh, Hal O'Brien, Cynthia Wan, Denis Coman, Brendan O'Donovan and Pat Farrell. Frankfort Avenue resident Michael Barry must be commended for his landmark work, *Victorian Dublin Revealed.* Also, Peter Pearson's *Decorative Dublin* and Mary Daly, Mona Hearn and Peter Pearson's *Dublin's Victorian Houses* were of particular help. Profound gratitude to Angela MacNamara (former resident), whose reminiscences captured the atmosphere of 1930s Rathgar so well. As did 'Thank Heavens We Are Living in Rathgar', by Jimmy O'Dea and Harry O'Donovan. The late and indefatigable Fred E. Dixon was also a great inspiration. He did much over the years to methodically chronicle a history of Rathgar. His extensive work on Rathgar now resides with the Dublin City Archives on Pearse Street. Laetitia Lefroy helped greatly with old photos of Faunagh House on Orwell Road. Thanks to The Rambling House for information on Peggy Jordan and to John Byrne of Byrne's Family Butchers, Seán Cronin of the Gourmet Shop and the Davy Group for information on the history of the company. Another local, Angela O'Connell, has done much work on the Rathmines Township and the Three Patrons' church. Grateful thanks also to Séamus Ó Maitiú for his Rathmines and Rathgar Township works. Mary Doyle of Ardagh House was most accommodating. The extraordinary and helpful Ulick O'Connor was kindness in itself in sharing his memories of Rathgar, as was former resident, Angela MacNamara. The dynamic Rathgar Residents' Association has done much sterling work to protect and enhance Rathgar and was most forthcoming, particularly individuals such as John McCarthy, Mark McDowell and Barbara Fleming. The Rathmines, Rathgar and Ranelagh History Society and the Rathmines and Rathgar Musical Society were also helpful. Thanks to the *Irish Independent*'s Mark Keenan for information on some of the history of Clarendon. To estate agents Sherry Fitzgerald, Douglas Newman Good, and Savill's, a big thanks! The Parish Development and Renewal Core Group, the Parish Priest, Fr Joseph Mullan, Frs Sammon and Commane and the parishioners of the Church of the Three Patrons, have worked hard to make their church a splendid and welcoming place. Likewise, much gratitude to the personnel of Christ Church, Zion Road church, Grosvenor Road and Brighton Road churches, as well as Leicester Avenue synagogue. Thanks to Libby McElroy of Trinity Hall and to Kate Palmer of Trinity College. Thanks to Bewley's Café for information on the early days. Other residents, including Sharon Griffin, Michael McGarry, Helen Rock, and John McKiernan, were inspiring. Heartfelt thanks to Reggie Redmond and St Luke's Hospital for the history of Oakland (Rathgar House) and to the librarian Marie Corrigan. Also to Elizabeth Birdthistle of *The Irish Times* for information on Kenilworth Road. Pat Fennell of Highfield Grove was helpful with information on the tramway cottages. Frances and Malachy Coleman of Kenilworth Square have done much to preserve a beautiful house and made a big effort to help me. Many thanks also to David Kerr for his history of the Rathgar National School and to the staff and former pupils of that school. David Robbins and Peter Costello were inspiring on James Joyce. And Pat Comerford's musings are always helpful. Thanks to Jacolet for her nineteenth-century photos. Ronan Colgan and Beth Amphlett of The History Press Ireland were most encouraging and patient and for this I am very grateful. Finally, a hearty thanks to the businesses and residents of Rathgar for ensuring that this unique and historic area of Dublin offers such a wonderful and welcoming experience.

INTRODUCTION

Rathgar is a quiet leafy south Dublin suburb just 3km from Grafton Street. It consists approximately of the area bounded on the south by the River Dodder, on the north by Rathmines and Dartry, on the east by Milltown Golf Club and Churchtown and the west by Rathfarnham/Terenure and Harold's Cross Roads. The name Rathgar derives from the Irish *Ráth Garbh*, meaning 'rough ringfort'. Rath's were early Gaelic defensive structures usually built on elevated land to command views of the surrounding area. The one in Rathgar was located in the Highfield Road area, in the vicinity of what are now Templemore, Neville and Villiers roads. John Taylor's map of the environs of Dublin in 1816 shows an earthen ringfort situated in this vicinity.

This is a most fascinating area in Dublin – full of history, mystery and magic. Today, the housing stock largely comprises red-brick late Georgian and Victorian terraces and much of the area lies within an architectural conservation zone. This is not surprising since many houses have Greek, Gothic, Georgian, Victorian or Edwardian influences. The architectural experimentation of the mid-nineteenth century had climaxed by the 1860s and the fruits of that era are to be found in Rathgar. Some of Dublin's most impressive roads and dwellings, churches, schools and other fine buildings are to be found here.

It is an area that has for centuries attracted some of the most influential people in Dublin (and Irish) political, social, business and professional, cultural and literary life. Many of these people have had a profound influence on every aspect of Irish society. Moreover and uniquely, four Nobel Prize winners either lived in Rathgar or had connections with it. Individuals such as James Joyce, author of *Ulysses*, who was born in Rathgar, George Russell (Æ), W.B. Yeats, Arnold Bax and other members of the Rathgar Circle put the area on the map, as did Maud Gonne. Other great writers, including Bram Stoker, J.M. Synge, David Marcus and William Carleton, lived in Rathgar.

Businessmen such as Charles Wisdom Hely, Frederick Stokes, David Drummond, Charles Eason of Eason's bookshops, the Davy brothers and Ernest Bewley of Bewley's Cafés lived in Rathgar for many years. The founders/owners/managers of some of Dublin's great department stores, including Clerys, Brown Thomas and Arnotts, have lived there. Newspaper owners and editors, including Douglas Gageby of *The Irish Times*, also resided there. Some of Ireland's greatest nineteenth-century architects, such as George Palmer Beater, either built there or lived there (or both). Ireland's foremost twentieth-century artist Louis Le Brocquy also resided in Rathgar. Some of Ireland's greatest thespians – Siobhán McKenna, Denis O'Dea, Jimmy O'Dea and Maureen Potter – either lived there or had connections with the area. The legendary Jimmy O'Dea was so enthralled by the area that he came out with the song 'Thank Heavens We Are Living in Rathgar'!

Senior politicians and future presidents, such as Erskine Childers (both senior and junior; the latter became President of Ireland), former Taoisigh Séan Lemass and Jack Lynch worked and lived there, as did Ernest Blythe. Activists involved in the 1916 Rising and the War of Independence lived and met in Rathgar, including Thomas MacDonagh, Eoin MacNeill and Michael Collins.

Rathgar village in the early twentieth century. (Courtesy of GCI)

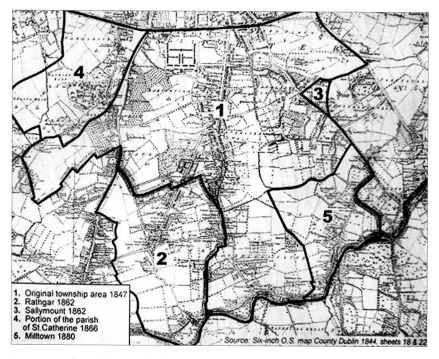

1. Original township area 1847
2. Rathgar 1862
3. Sallymount 1862
4. Portion of the parish of St.Catherine 1866
5. Milltown 1880

Source: Six-inch O.S. map County Dublin 1844, sheets 18 & 22

Late nineteenth-century map of Rathmines Townships showing Rathgar at No. 2.
(Courtesy of Ordnance Survey Office)

Veterans of the War of Independence, such as Countess Markievicz, Dan Breen, Ned Broy and Patrick O'Hegarty, lived there. Another Nobel Prize winner, Ernest Walton, also lived there. As did William Martin Murphy of 1913 infamy.

The influence of the Normans, the Reformation, Cromwell and the Battle of Rathmines in 1649, the 1798 Rebellion, the 1913 Dublin Lockout, 1916 and the War of Independence: Rathgar featured in all of these chapters of history.

This unique district in Dublin has such a rich and impressive history that this book can only serve as an introduction to an area that has created a lasting influence on so many people.

1

EARLY HISTORY, THE CASTLE AND THE CUSACK FAMILY

Prior to the Norman invasion of Ireland in the twelfth century, the lands of Rathgar were part of the home farm, or grange, of the Augustinian nuns of the Abbey of St Mary, whose convent stood at College Green, Dublin. The order had been established by Dermot Mac Murrough, High King of Leinster, in the middle of the twelfth century. The name Rathgar has been in continuous use since the thirteenth century and was used to describe the area containing a rath (fortification) in the vicinity of the farm, in what is now called Highfield.

For hundreds of years the lands of Rathgar containing this outlying 90-acre farm continued to prosper under the nuns. However, with the Dissolution of the Monasteries during Henry VIII's Reformation, the lands were seized and granted to Nicholas Segrave in 1539. Later, in the early 1600s, the occupant of these lands, consisting now of more than 120 acres, was Alderman John Cusack, who was Mayor of Dublin in 1608.[1]

THE CUSACKS AND CROMWELL

The Cusack family bought the lands and the manor house for use as a country residence. John Cusack was Mayor of Dublin in 1608 and was head of one of Dublin's oldest and leading mercantile families, having substantial trade dealings with England. He was an alderman from 1604 until his death in 1626. He was from a long-settled and prominent family in Co. Meath that had strong connections with similarly prosperous families. During these years the family resided at the manor house and what had become known as Rathgar Castle. Its location was in the immediate vicinity of what is now Highfield Road. The most reliable authorities place the site of the castle in the area immediately south of the upper end of Rathgar Road (44–49 Highfield Road and near Fairfield Park).

The house was sacked during the important Battle of Rathmines in 1649, in which the parliamentarian garrison of Dublin defeated the Royalist army under the Duke of Ormonde. Oliver Cromwell's forces, under Colonel Michael Jones, on landing in Dublin at Ringsend, had captured Baggotrath Castle. The defenders retreated, but Jones cut them off by marching his army along the Dodder, past Donnybrook, and then swinging around to meet the Royalists at the Battle of Rathmines. The defeated army of over 2,000 soldiers fled to the woods near Rathgar Castle and a number of the soldiers actually took up residence in the castle. This was an ideal position for the army to camp, given its elevated position. Unfortunately, however, this did not suit the Cusacks and they obtained orders forbidding the Royalist troops from cutting timber in the wood and taking their horses and carts while drawing corn from their fields.

Amongst the Royalist troops holding Rathgar Castle, some defected to the opposition. According to a contemporary witness, some of the Royalist forces

Rathgar Road in the early twentieth century. (Courtesy of GCI)

'who, after some defence, obtained conditions for their lives, and the next day most of them took up arms in our service'. Following the success of his forces at the Battle of Rathmines, Oliver Cromwell was then able to sweep through Leinster and rout the rest of the Irish forces with much bloodshed.

Following the upheaval, the Cusacks, being Protestants of the Calvinist persuasion, were allowed to retain Rathgar Castle, which they repaired and continued to live in. In the Hearth Rolls of 1664 'Rathgar Castle' was said to have had five hearths, a sign of prosperity and comfort. In the early 1670s Cusack's second son Adam took over the castle when his original heir, Robert, died in the latter part of the seventeenth century. He had considerable influence as he was by marriage a nephew of Sir Maurice Eustace, the Lord Chancellor. He died in 1681. His widow and family continued to live in the castle.[2]

Historian Nicholas Donnelly, writing in 1908 about the Catholic Parish of Rathgar, noted that after the upheavals John Cusack was living in Rathgar Castle with Alice, his wife, his eldest son John, his daughter, two menservants and two maidservants, one described as 'a full fat wench'.[3]

The castle remained in the Cusacks' possession for at least a century, but during the mid-eighteenth century the property fell into ruin. The extensive ruins were still standing at the end of the eighteenth century, but they had deteriorated greatly over the years. In 1782 only the walls of a large and

Cattle grazing in the grounds of ruins of Rathgar Castle, 1769. (Courtesy of NLI/RIA)

extensive building, the remains of several outhouses and an entrance gateway remained. The lands were rented out to market gardeners, dairymen and to various people, including one Henry Coulson, whose name lives on in Coulson Avenue.

Paintings of later years, however, show the castle in ruins, including one in the National Gallery by the artist C.M. Campbell and another by Gabriel Beranger, a Dutch Huguenot living in Ireland, of 1769.

In 1782, the well-known antiquarian, Austin Cooper, visited the area and described how he found only the walls and an entrance gateway still standing. Geoghegan, the author of a book of ballads *The Monks of Kilcrea*, described the ruins in his poem 'The Rapparee's Tale':

> Rathgar, upon thy broken wall,
> Now grows the lusmore rank and tall –
> Wild grass upon thy hearthstone springs,
> And ivy round thy turret clings;
> The night-owls through thy arches sweep,
> Thy moat dried up, thy towers a heap,
> Blackened, and charr'd and desolate –
> The traveller marvels at thy fate!
>
> But other look thy tall towers bore
> Upon that well known night,
> When silentlie we scaled the bawn
> And stood beneath thy tall oak boughs,
> Close sheltered from the sight
> With bustle loud thy courtyards rung
> As horseman from their saddles sprung
> All lightly to the ground.[4]

In 1784 the remaining structures suffered again during an attack by a number of the United Irishmen Volunteers who were only driven out of it with great difficulty.

Taylor's Map of 1816 shows the ruins near Highfield Road and St Luke's Hospital. The word 'ruins' is also visible on a 1909 map of Rathgar close to this location. The lane or bridle track to it is now Rathgar Avenue, the oldest road in the locality. Highfield Road is much newer; it was laid out in 1753 to connect the old castle of Rathmines with Terenure and Rathfarnham. It was originally just a farm lane leading to and from Rathmines Castle, located near the present-day Palmerston Park. Originally called Cross Avenue, it was later called Highfield Road.

The Ordnance Survey Map of 1837 shows that there was a house near the site of the castle ruins called 'Rathgar Castle Cottage' – a name which was probably intended to commemorate the nearness to the site of the castle, whose ruins may have survived in the memory of the builder. Interestingly, a Rathgar Cottage still stands at 124 Rathgar Road and dates from the 1840s. It is probable that it stands on the site of the original castle cottage. However, to confuse matters, across from this house, at 103 Rathgar Road, there is a dwelling called 'Castle Cottage'!

The area opened up in the mid-eighteenth century when a new road (Highfield) was constructed. Near the ruins of the old Rathgar Castle, a family known as the Wilsons built a house called Rathgar House.[5]

2

PLEASANT HOUSES AND DETACHED VILLAS, 1750–1850

For more than one hundred years after the Battle of Rathmines, Rathgar remained a rural area with just a few large residences. However, a village gradually developed, firstly because it was a junction where the new Highfield Road met Rathgar Avenue and secondly to cater for the needs of Rathgar Castle and subsequently the large residences nearby.

One of oldest houses in Rathgar, on Rathgar Avenue. Notice the loft over the garage doors. (Courtesy of DNG)

Despite this gradual development, Rathgar remained very much a rural idyll until the 1740s. A lot of the land remained under cultivation and was used by market gardeners and dairymen to graze their cattle. Names recalling the rural nature of Rathgar are still commemorated by the likes of Highfield, Ashgrove and Oaklands. A significant transformation in the mid-1750s due to the construction of Highfield Road, which linked Dublin city and Rathmines to Rathfarnham. As soon as the road was built, houses followed.

RATHGAR HOUSE AND 1798

It has been suggested that the first house built in Rathgar, after Rathgar Castle, was Oakland, known originally as Rathgar House and built in *c.* 1780 on Cross Avenue, later Highfield Road. The house, built for the Wilson family, was described as being 'in the heart of the country'. A prominent Dublin solicitor, Charles Farren, later owned it towards the end of the eighteenth century (most likely the early 1780s). The Farren family lived there until the mid-nineteenth century. A prominent individual in Dublin legal circles, Farren's presence in Rathgar must have generated interest in the area. His house was the first modern house built there.[6]

However, the house was still isolated and in 1798 it was the scene of an attack which saw an employee, Daniel Carroll, who lived in a gate lodge on the estate, murdered. The *Freeman's Journal* of 17 March 1798 described the attack:

> Yesterday morning, about two o'clock, a numerous banditti, said to be forty in number, attacked the country house of Charles Farren, Esq., which is situated adjoining the avenue that leads to Rathfarnham Road. They cruelly put [Carroll] to death ...[7]

Three of the attackers were subsequently arrested, charged and executed at the nearby Terenure crossroads in late October. The *Freeman's Journal* described the route of the execution procession from Kilmainham Jail. It passed Highfield Road and Rathgar House. It reported that 'the bloody shirt of poor Carroll was placed in front of the cart before them [those found guilty] on the way to the place of execution. After hanging the usual time, they were cut down and their bodies conveyed to the Surgeons' Hall for dissection, consonant to the letter of the law.'[8]

The repercussions of the 1798 Rebellion were still affecting the country a year later. Charles Farren wrote to his daughter in England saying the country was quiet owing to the uncompromising response of the government in 1798 'in punishing those offenders daily brought to justice for their atrocious crimes. Scarce a day passes but one of two of those deluded wretches are executed or sent to the King of Prussia to serve in his armies.'[9]

Farren died in 1808 and the house was passed on to this son Joseph, also a clerk of the Pleas at the Court of Exchequer. He did much to improve and develop Rathgar House. He also leased some land from a nearby landlord, known as Lodge, who held the title of Baron Frankfort (hence Frankfort Avenue). The Farren family sold the property after Joseph's death in 1853. His two daughters moved to Georgeville (16 Highfield Road) and died at the end of the 1890s.

TODD BURNS AND BROWN THOMAS

The new purchaser of Rathgar House was the wealthy businessman Henry Walker Todd of the famous Todd, Burns & Co. Drapers, established in 1834. Gilbert Burns was a nephew of the Scottish poet, Robert Burns. A major

Zion Road Church of Ireland
church. (Courtesy of NLI)

investor in the company was Alexander Findlater, an importer of wines and spirits whose company later became a household name in certain prosperous suburbs of Dublin, including Rathgar.

The name Rathgar House was changed to Oakland by the family. It is thought the reason for the name change was because there were two other properties in the area with the same name. There is still a property on Bushy Park Road called Rathgar House. The Todds, however, did not stay long in Oakland as H.W. Todd died in 1863 and two years later the house and fourteen acres were sold. The new owner was Hugh Brown, who had worked in the Todd Burns emporium on Mary Street. He opened his own business in 1849 and formed the well-known Brown Thomas store on Grafton Street with another businessman. When he moved to Rathgar in the 1860s, the area was known as 'one of the most prestigious and desirable places to live'. He died in 1882. One of his sons, Robert, a doctor, lived at Hopeton, a large and distinctive house at 33 Terenure Road East. He is remembered in one of the stained-glass windows in the chancel of Zion Road church: 'To the glory of God and in loving memory of Robert Browne M.D. of Hopeton, Rathgar who died on Apl. 29th 1913'. One of Brown's daughters, Marianne, lived in Oakland for another ten years after her father's death, until she moved to her newly built house at 1 Zion Road (called Glengyle and now Stratford College).[10]

THE HELY COAT OF ARMS

Towards the end of 1893, the house was bought by another businessman, Charles Wisdom Hely of the stationary and printing company with premises on Dame Street. He began to develop and improve Oakland and to make his new home one of the most significant in the south Dublin suburbs. He added a new wing, a billiard room and a large ballroom. Moreover, the dining room, sitting room and drawing room were re-decorated with silk tapestry and he had the ceilings painted by a specially commissioned Italian artist. These beautiful ceilings may still be seen today in what is now the library. Across the finely decorated hall is the present-day Boardroom, also noteworthy, not only for the mural on the ceiling, but also for the magnificent fireplace and mantelpiece, half-timbered walls and the hardwood flooring – all originals.

Seven servants, including a governess and a butler, looked after the needs of the new household. Hely had a croquet lawn, tennis courts, a putting green, a rock garden and ponds installed in the vicinity of the house. Four gardeners looked after the grounds and the heated glasshouses contained fruit and vegetables for the house. Today, the grounds are still impressive and there is an original small original wooded area containing ancient trees and paths to amble about on.

He acquired extra land in Orwell Park, which gave him a second entrance to his property (the first being on Highfield Road). He enhanced this new rear entrance with fine pillars and wrought-iron gates, on which he had his initials carved. Today we can still see CWH and an arm holding a broken spear (part of his crest) on the gates to what is now St Luke's Hospital. The Lodge at this entrance similarly has his crest and the date of construction – 1893. His crest and coat of arms can also be seen on the stained-glass window in the house. The family's motto, 'Certavi et Vici' ('I have fought and conquered'), is emblazoned on this window. Hely acquired land at nearby Sunbury and leased it to the Mount Temple Lawn Tennis Club. He had access to the club via his own private gate.

Hely became one of the first owners of a motor car in Rathgar when he bought a seven-horsepower Panhard in 1901. It had a top speed of 30mph. His purchase was covered in the weekly magazine *Motor News* and the May edition for 1902 had an article 'Mr C. Wisdom Hely and His Motor Stud'. The article noted that on arriving in Dublin with his new car he 'was already an expert and drove at a pace through traffic which terrified the onlookers and left the police aghast'. However, the article reassured its readers that Hely 'has now covered between 5,000 and 10,000 miles without causing any accident of any description'. It also noted that Hely intended to use his car 'largely for running down to his fishing in the Mayo highlands. The distance is over 200 miles, and he expects to find it a comfortable day's journey.'[11]

Hely died in 1929 and his wife, Edith Mary, continued to live in the house. In 1936 she sold some of the land bordering the avenue leading from Highfield Road to the house to a builder. This is now Oakland Drive. The impressive entrance gates were removed and placed in their present location at Orwell Park. The family owned the house until 1950 when it sold it to the Cancer Association of Ireland and it became St Luke's Hospital, which it has remained to this day.[12]

NURSERIES AND MILLS

There were a number of businesses developing in Rathgar at this time – Grimwood's Nurseries at a site on what is now Kenilworth Road and Grosvenor

Road; Dartry Dye Works; Waldron's Calico Mills on Orwell Road Bridge; and Rathgar Quarry and its windmill on the site of the present-day Herzog Park.

Taylor's Map for 1816 shows the early outline of Rathgar, with the five main roads extending out from the village. The map also shows quarries, Grimwood's Nursery and the printworks and mill, but very few houses in Rathgar. There were none on Rathgar Road, only Rathgar House on Highfield Road and a few smaller dwellings on Rathgar Avenue and Orwell Road near the crossroads. A house, Annedale, and a few cottages are shown on Dartry Road. For the next 200 years Rathgar developed around this skeleton.

Over the next few decades a few more houses appeared and the *Dublin Almanac* for 1835 had nearly sixty dwellings listed for Rathgar. The new elegant villa and terraced houses were in the Regency style, with fanlights and pillared front doorways, which were at the top of a flight of steps with railings. The first terrace in Rathgar was Spire View in 1834. The name derived from the view of Holy Trinity church in nearby Rathmines. Other terraces were Alma and Malakoff, at the Rathmines end of Rathgar Road, names inspired by the Crimean War. For many years residents in Rathgar used the name of the house or a number in the short terrace of three to four houses rather than a particular road number, e.g. 1 Francesca Terrace (along Grosvenor Road). The numbering of the houses on the main roads of Rathgar began in 1866 on Rathgar Road. Terenure Road East was not finished until the 1930s and Dartry Road not until the 1950s.[13]

Samuel Lewis's *Topographical Dictionary of Ireland* for 1837, described Rathgar as:

a district, which is on the road from Dublin, by way of Rathmines, to Roundtown, consists of several ranges of pleasant houses and numerous detached villas, of which the principal are Rathgar House, the residence of J. Farran, Esq.; Rathgar, of P. Waldron, Esq.; Rokeby, of C. Pickering, Esq.; Mote View, of J. Powell, Esq.; Mountain Prospect, of P. Nolan, Esq.; Roseville, of Miss Moore; Fair View, of Mrs. Fox; Prospect Villa, of J. Houston, Esq.; Maryville, of J. Jennings, Esq.; Prospect Lodge, of R. Clarke, Esq.; Primrose Cottage, of T. Alley, Esq.; and the handsome residences of G. Wall and W. Haughton, Esqrs. There is an extensive bleach-green, with printing-works belonging to Messrs. Waldron, Dodd, Carton, & Co., for muslin, calicoes, and silks; the works are set in motion by a steam-engine of 30-horse power, and a water-wheel of equal force, and afford employment to 300 men. In the immediate vicinity are some quarries of good limestone, which are extensively worked; and strata of calp limestone have been discovered alternating with the limestone in several places, here, as well as in the quarries at Roundtown and Crumlin, inclined at a considerable angle and exhibiting other appearances of disturbance.

This is a good summary of some of the activities and people of Rathgar in the early nineteenth century, with 'pleasant houses and detached villas'. Many of these are still visible and distinctive in Rathgar, although they are now surrounded by modern buildings.[14]

3

RATHGAR AND THE TOWNSHIP, 1847–1862

THE FLIGHT FROM THE CITY ACROSS THE CANALS

The growth of residential areas away from the central shopping, commercial and industrial core of a city was a common phenomenon in the nineteenth and early twentieth century across Europe. Dublin was no exception. In part the move to the suburbs was a flight of wealth. At the end of the eighteenth century, the spacious streets at the centre of the city were dominated by a moneyed lifestyle at odds with the squalor of the poorer population. In the south of the city, from St Stephen's Green through Merrion Square and Fitzwilliam Square, great Georgian houses were homes for many of the nobility, the gentry and the higher professions. On the north side, Mountjoy Square and Rutland Square, as well as fashionable streets, such as Henrietta Street and North Great Georges Street, were home to many leading members of the legal, ecclesiastical and business communities.

The nineteenth century saw many wealthy Dubliners move to suburbs such as Rathmines, Monkstown and Blackrock as many in the professional classes sought residences at a distance from the polluted, overcrowded city centre. But not everyone who could afford to moved to the suburbs: for example, Fitzwilliam Square and Merrion Square on the south side remained the preserve of the wealthy. This was a world of doctors, dentists, top civil servants, lawyers and army officers. The old fashionable districts of the north side, however, were almost entirely abandoned. Among the starkest examples were the great buildings of Henrietta Street, which became

Nineteenth-century map of the townships of Dublin. (Courtesy of GCI)

tenements. This also happened at Mountjoy Square (and nearby Monto) and Parnell Square.[15]

This relocation was to some extent driven by the growth of the middle classes, who desired houses that would reflect their new status, houses which could not be provided within the confines of the city limits. Development of such suburbs was driven by businessmen and property developers, as in the case of Rathgar.

The impetus for the development of Rathgar was in fact the growth of the neighbouring district of Rathmines. From the 1860s Rathmines grew year after year. The most sustained house-building took place in the 1860s and it was in this decade that we really see the growth of Rathgar. The increasingly congested condition of Rathmines had forced house-seekers who were looking for suburban residences to look further afield. The easy and frequent transport to the city centre, first by omnibuses and then by trams, soon added Rathgar to the domain of villadom and encouraged developers to open up avenues, roads and squares. And so it did not take long to attract people to Rathgar.[16]

However, there were also other pertinent factors responsible for the development of Rathgar. As far back as 1828 an Act of Parliament made it easy to establish a local authority to provide basic services such as public lighting, some policing, street paving, building sewers and drains, providing water services and keeping a fire engine. This and further local government acts, combined with the entrepreneurship of property developers such as Frederick Stokes, greatly facilitated the growth of suburbs such as Rathgar.[17]

Furthermore, according to Mary Daly's study of the growth of Victorian Dublin, it was probably no coincidence that Rathmines Township was established in 1847 when the Great Famine was at its peak or that a record number of families moved to the suburbs, including Rathgar, during the 1860s, a decade marked by epidemics of smallpox and cholera in Dublin's city centre.

The establishment of the Dublin Townships from the 1840s onwards greatly encouraged more people to move out of the city and into the suburbs. Townships were like small towns, each with their own town hall and commissioners (called councillors today). They were entrusted to look after issues such as roads, lighting, sewerage, drainage and water.

With the creation of the Rathmines Urban Township in 1847, ostensibly because of the poor state of the roads, the demand for houses among Dublin's middle classes (mainly Anglo-Irish Protestant and Unionist), who sought a safe and healthy environment and a home that was sufficiently close to the city to commute by walking, grew exponentially. Many saw the township as an opportunity to preserve the Protestant Unionist way of life and identity, particularly at a time when the growth of Irish nationalism was challenging their place in Irish society.[18]

THE EARLY DAYS OF THE RATHMINES AND RATHGAR TOWNSHIP

The development of Rathgar cannot be viewed in isolation from Rathmines. The Rathmines Township was created in 1847 by an Act of Parliament. Its chairman was Frederick Stokes, an Englishman who lived in Monkstown. He had been involved in several businesses but decided to become a speculative builder. *Plus ça change, plus c'est la même chose!* To quote Séamas Ó Maitiú: 'The most promising area for the activities of speculative property developers was Rathmines and adjoining districts.'[19]

Initially the township was created as a sanitary area but new functions were added over time and the township became responsible for public lighting, water supply, drainage and the erection of a number of small housing schemes.[20]

THE ADDITION OF RATHGAR TO THE TOWNSHIP 1862

In 1852 the residents of Rathgar agreed that the Rathmines Township should be extended to include Rathgar. The following year local landowner Sir Robert Shaw of Bushy Park House, Terenure, lent his weight to a delegation to press for inclusion. However, they were faced with formidable opposition from Rathmines Township businessmen, including Frederick Stokes. According to the powerful and influential Stokes, Rathgar had nothing in common with Rathmines. He argued, successfully, that it was a different electoral division for poor law rates and consequently paid 50 per cent more than Rathmines; it was a different parish for ecclesiastical rates, a different barony for county rates. Moreover, it was only half the size of Rathmines but had more than half the length of road to be maintained and it was less than a quarter of the valuation. He also pointed out that Rathgar residents might be hostile to the present Rathmines Township commissioners and could try to oust them. Such was Stokes' influence that the matter was dropped for a number of years. However, when the matter arose again, Rathgar residents agreed to Stokes' demands that they cover financial costs involved in the amalgamation. The move went ahead and in 1862 the important extension took place. Under the Rathmines and Rathgar Improvement Act, Rathgar was added to the township and it was renamed the Rathmines and Rathgar Township.[21]

The new district was to be a separate ward with three members representing it on the board of the Rathmines and Rathgar Township. Three wealthy Rathgar businessmen – George Sykes, Maxwell McMaster and Henry W. Todd – took their seats on the Rathmines and Rathgar Township Board. The new development had an immediate and positive impact on Rathgar. The population in the 1861 census for Rathgar was 1,806. This nearly doubled in the next twenty years, with new roads and houses being built.

The new dwellings of Rathgar were generally of a good standard. There was the typical red-brick Victorian house, both small and large, to cater for all budgets. On the bigger roads the houses were built in either terraces or as one-offs and this can still be clearly seen. They also built large Gothic Revival (Grosvenor Road) and Greek Revival (Kenilworth) houses. Of course the names chosen for the roads in the area were intended to tempt the more Anglo-aligned hearts of would-be purchasers. At one stage there was a proposal to change the name from Rathgar to Garville![22]

Rathgar was described in 1872 as 'a Townland with a population of 1,180 and having greatly improved within the last few years it is now one of the most pleasing outlets of Dublin, being studded with terraces of good houses and detached villas'.[23]

CANAL WATER AND CHAMBER POTS

Originally the township was governed by commissioners, but under the Local Government (Ireland) Act of 1898 the Rathmines and Rathgar Urban District Council was established as the elected governing body. The township was initially created as a sanitary area, but new functions were added by various acts, so that its duties came to include most functions of local government. It shared responsibility with the Pembroke Township.

The main incentive to living in the area was that it had lower rates. However, the lack of an adequate water supply for the rapidly growing Rathgar was a regular source of complaint. Dublin Corporation was willing to supply water, but at a cost, thereby increasing rates. There was a disastrous scheme to use canal water. Robert Mallet was commissioned to investigate the feasibility of the River Dodder (which flowed through Rathgar) as a possible source of usable water as early as 1844. The township water tower was built in 1872 and was located on a lane off Brighton Road, Rathgar. This lane is now called Tower Avenue, after the tower. The tank was sixty feet above the tallest house in the area and held over 100,000 gallons. The water came from the Grand Canal at Harold's Cross Bridge and was pumped into the tank at night. Dodder water finally ran into the township in 1878, but for many years, adequate water provision was a major issue in Rathgar. Initially there was sometimes great difficulty providing water to houses in areas such as Highfield Road because of their elevation.[24]

The former lane, Tower Avenue, is just one of the many long lanes that are a feature of Rathgar and the surrounding Victorian areas. Before the installation of toilets and bathrooms in these houses, residents had to use outdoor facilities: a privy at the end of the back garden. At night, the 'night soil' men would collect the contents of chamber pots which the housemaid had emptied into a cesspit in the garden. The 'night men' would do their work via the back lanes of the houses. On no account would they enter through the front doors. Many houses in Rathgar did not have indoor bathrooms until well into the 1890s. In addition, despite the advent of gas lighting, candles and oil lamps were used in most houses until the early twentieth century and even then the demand for gas was slow to grow. It was not until 1907–8 that residents of Rathgar, beginning with Highfield Road, started to use gas for heating and cooking. House-building at this time reflected the new trend: nowadays on Highfield Road or Brighton Road, one sees the older three-storey houses with basements on one side of the road and the newer two-storey houses on the opposite side.[25]

MRS BEETON'S SERVANTS

The vast majority of houses in Rathgar had at least one domestic servant looking after the households needs. The size of the houses and the social aspirations of the residents necessitated servants. The number of servants per house varied. In Kenilworth Square in 1901, for example, of the 101 houses in the area, only three had four servants, whereas fifty-nine had one, twenty had two and eighteen had none. Residents looked to Mrs Beeton's Victorian household management book for guidance on the roles of servants. Titles ranged from 'maid-of-all-work', in situations where there was only one servant who did practically everything in the house, to housemaid, parlour maid and cook for the bigger houses. It was not until the 1920s that the benefits of electricity began to be felt and the need for domestic servants was reappraised.[26]

FOUR-FACED LIAR

The urban district council (UDC) used to meet in the magnificent town hall on Rathmines Road, which was designed by Sir Thomas Drew. It was used for the first meeting of the council in January 1899. The interior fittings were by Carlo Cambi of Siena, who was also responsible for doors and panelling in the National Library and the National Museum of Ireland. The famous town hall clock (often called 'the four-faced liar') was made in 1897 by Chancellor and Son of Bachelor's Walk and Sackville Street (modern-day O'Connell Street) at a cost of £130. The clock chimes were also made in 1897, by Matthew Byrne of James's Street, at a cost of £264.

The centre of Rathgar, c. 1900. (Courtesy of Rathgar Presbyterian Church)

The township survived until well into the twentieth century when its administration was taken over by Dublin City Council under the Local Government (Dublin) Act of 1930. The UDC held its last meeting in the town hall in 1930 and today the building is the Rathmines Senior College.[27]

4

TRAMS AND TRANSPORT –
THE VULTURE OF DARTRY HALL

The early development of trams in Dublin saw an initial proposal to lay out a railway from the city to Rathgar and thence to Rathcoole. The city terminus was to be on Trinity Street. The bill, promoted in Parliament, actually reached the committee stage in 1865 but failed to pass. One of the arguments made in its favour was the potential suburban traffic. The proposed railway had the resounding title of the Rathmines, Rathgar and Rathcoole Railway.

Until 1863 the only routes to the Churchtown area were very indirect – either by Classon's Bridge, near Dartry, or by Rathfarnham. Soon after this date Orwell (originally Waldron's) Bridge was completed and led to the slow development of this part of Rathgar.

Built by the Dublin Tramways Company, the tram service was inaugurated in early 1872 and ran from College Green to Garville Avenue. Such was the success of this development that further lines were added in subsequent years and trams travelled to different parts of Rathgar, including Kenilworth Square, Rathgar Road and Dartry Road. The numbers 14 and 15 trams serviced the area.[28]

TRAMYARDS, HAZARDS AND DIAMONDS

At the junction of Dartry Road and Orwell Park, there stands a striking structure – Tramway House, the former terminus and depot for the No. 14 tram from Nelson's Pillar on Dublin's O'Connell Street to Dartry. The exterior is

The No. 15 tram from Nelson's Pillar to Rathmines and Dartry. (Courtesy of the Howth Transport Museum)

The Dublin United Tramways Company (1896), Ltd.

ROUTES

NELSON'S PILLAR
TO
DALKEY
TO
TERENURE
TO
SANDYMOUNT
TO
PALMERSTON PARK

RATHFARNHAM
TO
DRUMCONDRA

DONNYBROOK
TO
PHŒNIX PARK

O'CONNELL BRIDGE
TO
PARKGATE

KENILWORTH SQUARE
TO
LANSDOWNE RD.

ROUTES.

NELSON'S PILLAR
TO
HOWTH
TO
SANDYMOUNT
TO
DARTRY ROAD
TO
CLONSKEA

DOLPHIN'S BARN
TO
GLASNEVIN

HATCH STREET
TO
KINGSBRIDGE

INCHICORE
TO
WESTLAND ROW

PARK GATE
TO
BALLYBOUGH

THE NELSON PILLAR.
The centre of Dublin Tramway System.

Directors :
WM. M. MURPHY, J.P., Chairman.
Ald. W. F. COTTON, J.P., D.L., M.P.; JOSEPH MOONEY, J.P.;
CAPT. C. COLTHURST VESEY, D.L.

Secretary :
R. S. TRESILIAN, A.M.I.C.E.I., F.C.I.S.

Manager :
C. W. GORDON.

Offices: 9 UPPER SACKVILLE STREET, DUBLIN.

A poster showing the routes of the Dublin United Tramways Company of which William Martin Murphy was a director. (Courtesy of Howth Transport Museum) reminiscent of that bygone tram era. The interior, now offices, is still open-plan and one can imagine the trams trundling in here at the end of their day's journey from Nelson's Pillar to Rathgar.

This terminus is only about 100 yards from the home of William Martin Murphy of Dartry Hall, Orwell Park. The house itself retains many of its distinctive and unusual features (e.g. a turret), although it has been adapted to modern usage. Murphy was the founder of the Dublin United Tramway Company (DUTC).

Before the advent of trams to Rathgar, residents used to commute via jaunting cars and hackney carriages in the early decades of the nineteenth century. From the mid-nineteenth century onwards they had an alternative – the horse-drawn omnibus, which left Rathgar crossroads each day with a scheduled on-the-hour service. There were a number of stands in Rathgar to cater for the variety of transport. These stands were also called 'hazards'. At Garville Avenue there was a hazard for two carriages. There was also a hazard at the Diamond opposite the Baptist church on Grosvenor Road and two at the Rathgar crossroads. There were strict rules as to the running of these stands or hazards. The horses' heads had to be facing a certain direction, the carriages had to rotate from stand to stand and the behaviour of the drivers had to be impeccable.[29]

In 1868 an advert in *The Irish Times*, hoping to encourage builders to set their sights on Brighton Square and Garville Avenue in Rathgar, stated that Mr Wilson's horse-drawn omnibuses passed every hour near Brighton Square.[30]

The Dublin Tramways Company inaugurated the city's first horse tram service from College Green to Garville Avenue, Rathgar, on 1 February 1872, the termini later becoming Nelson's Pillar and Terenure. This was a journey of twenty minutes in each direction with much cheaper fares than those paid on the horse omnibuses. Nonetheless travelling on the trams, in the early days at least, was a luxury only Dublin's white collar workers could afford. The majority of trams started or stopped at Nelson's Pillar.

The harness of the tram horses was trimmed with red facings to which little bells were attached. 'The inside of the cars,' the *Daily Express* noted, 'are richly cushioned in velvet and fitted with sliding shutters of Venetian glass type – the lamps are placed within ornamental coloured plate compart-ments ...' *The Irish Times* was less impressed: 'Only a pair of horses was provided for each tram, and these do not appear to be in breeding or stamina up to the work.' The tram service ran every six minutes. In 1881 three different tram companies amalgamated to form the Dublin United Tramway

Company (DUTC), which had 186 trams with over 1,000 horses. Horse trams were in operation until 1901.[31]

Electrification of the tram routes began in 1896 and the electric tram provided cheap and efficient service until the late 1940s. The gaily painted green-and-yellow trams with their garden seats, brass levers, crackling over-head cables and clanging bells became part of Dublin and Rathgar life. Every one of the four generations of Dublin trams – Open-top, Balcony, Standard and Luxury – was as characteristic of the city as the Custom House or the Ha'penny Bridge. The DUTC management and staff took special pride in the trams, which were built at Spa Road Works in Inchicore.[32]

The line through Rathgar was the number 15 Terenure line, whose termi-nus was Terenure crossroads. The number 14 route passed along the east side of Rathgar, with a terminus at Dartry and its tram sheds at Diamond Terrace nearby. A triangle of cottages for the workers on the number 14 route was built off Highfield Road.[33]

Behind Tramway House there is a cul-de-sac called Stable Lane. This is a rustic lane with an atmospheric old-style house called Ivy Villas, which is surrounded by towering trees. Nearby there is a converted old building called Holly Mews.

WILLIAM MARTIN MURPHY AND DARTRY HALL

William Martin Murphy's palatial home, Dartry Hall, was located just off Orwell Park. Its extensive grounds and tropical greenhouses stood in stark contrast to the homes of Dublin's working classes.

Murphy was closely associated with the house, having lived there since 1883. It featured in two cartoons published by the *Irish Worker* during the pro-tracted tram workers' strike, known as the 1913 Lockout. Both 'The Vulture of Dartry Hall' and 'William "Murder" Murphy's Dream of Conquest' depicted Murphy as a sinister presence at the gates of his estate with the deceased and injured poor of Dublin at his feet. He was a prominent Dublin businessman who owned Clerys Department Store, The *Irish Independent* and the DUTC, as well as the Imperial Hotel. He was director of many railway companies. He served as an MP for a time for Dublin. With his father-in-law, James Lombard, the nationalist MP, he helped to build many hundreds of houses all over Dublin.[34]

The vast Victorian house that was Dartry Hall (now Dartry House) is an imposing two-storey castellated mansion built in around 1810 with several

William Martin Murphy, who lived at Rostrevor Terrace then moved to Dartry Hall (House) Orwell Park. (Courtesy of NLI)

William Martin Murphy's palatial home, Dartry Hall, was located at Orwell Park, Rathgar. Its extensive grounds and tropical greenhouses were a stark contrast to the homes of Dublin's working classes. Murphy is closely associated with the house, having lived there since 1883. (Courtesy of the NLI)

James Adams, founder of Adam's Auctioneers, St Stephen's Green, lived for many years at Orwell Bank, Orwell Park. (Courtesy of Adam's Auctioneers)

additions made later, such as a Disneyesque turret, which was built in about 1900. The house was situated on a large piece of land, some of which was subsequently bought by the Mill Hill Fathers, who still retain a presence in the area (they too sold some of the land to builders in recent years). Today six of the impressive granite entrance pillars are still visible not too far from the house – four just off Orwell Road and two on Darty Road, near the Dye Works. They, and the house itself, are a reminder of the once powerful residents of the house. Its original owner was Obadiah Williams, a wealthy merchant of Huguenot origin. The house was owned by Dartry Mill owner William Wallace from 1844 to 1849 when it was bought by William Drury and kept in his family until 1888. From 1888 to 1958, the house was owned by the family of William Martin Murphy.

During the Dublin Lockout of 1913, employers locked out striking trade union members. The trade union side was led by Jim Larkin of the famous quotation, 'the great appear great because we are on our knees; let us arise'. Murphy, who was chairman of the Dublin Chamber of Commerce at the time, was the leader of the employers' side. Larkin described him as a 'capitalistic vampire'. Interestingly, there appears to have been more to Murphy than his business acumen, as he was a staunch Catholic and actively involved in

Cartoon, 1913, from the *Irish Worker* depicting William Martin Murphy outside his residence, Dartry Hall, Rathgar. (Courtesy of GCI)

Cartoon from the *Irish Worker* depicting William Martin Murphy outside Dartry Hall, Rathgar, as 'The Vulture of Dartry Hall'. (Courtesy of GCI)

the St Vincent de Paul Society and other charitable endeavours. He was also involved with the Milltown Golf Course, which Orwell Road cuts through.[35]

It is thought that Murphy was responsible for the majority of additions and extensions to the house, including the adding of a mansard attic floor and a turret form to the rear elevation.

He was succeeded in his businesses interests and at Dartry Hall by his son, William Lombard Murphy, and by Miss E. Murphy, who stayed on in the house after his death in 1919. During the Civil War in the early 1920s, the house was attacked because a member of the family was a pro-treaty councillor on the Rathmines and Rathgar Urban District Council.

The house was bought by the Mill Hill Fathers in the late 1950s. They, in turn, sold it in May 2005 to developer Eugene Renehan's Walthill Properties. It was converted into seven luxury properties and re-appeared on the market in 2013. The house is adjacent to the newly built houses on Orwell Park, on lands, including lawns and grounds that once belonged to the house that was known as Dartry Hall.[36]

5

THANK HEAVENS FOR RATHGAR – THE EXCLUSIVITY OF THE 1930s

STUBBORNLY MAINTAINING ITS EXCLUSIVITY – 'O THE SOLID, QUIET REFINEMENT OF RATHGAR'

Rathgar's image was solid, bourgeois and red-brick – cosy exclusiveness. This did not happen by accident as one of the main reasons for the growth of Rathgar in the late nineteenth century was that, according to the historian Séamus Ó Maitiú, '[t]he Victorians held the strong view that to re-inforce middle-class values, social segregation was necessary with the creation of single-class homogenous districts'.[37]

Consequently, there would be little room for 'inferior' housing stock in such areas. Many of the early residents would have been senior civil servants and officials in the Dublin Castle administration or public bodies and prosperous families that built villas, particularly on Rathgar Road. Brighton Road and Square were much farther out in the new suburb and so would have had more junior officials and less prosperous inhabitants.

COCKLES AND KNUCKLES

Long before the 1930s, Rathgar was regarded as being 'real posh'. Ireland's most famous comedian, actor and long-time Gaiety pantomime stalwart Jimmy O'Dea (1899–1965) created a popular catchphrase with his song, 'Thank Heavens We Are Living in Rathgar', which preserves the well-heeled

Rathgar image. It was written by his friend and colleague Harry O'Donovan. The lyrics went: 'There are some quite decent suburbs, I am sure. O Rathmines is not so bad or Terenure. In Dartry they are almost civilised. O we've heard of spots like Inchicore, but really don't know where they are. For, thank heavens, we are living in Rathgar.'[38]

The song noted that in the days of agitators and dictatorships, schisms and other isms (the world of the 1930s), one never knew who one was talking to. One might meet plumbers at golf dinners and at rugby dances one's finer sensibilities would be shocked by vulgar glances. Consequently the people of Rathgar were 'more danced against than dancing'. Luckily and despite all these challenges, the people of Rathgar had their evening dinners where vulgar politics was never discussed. The song also bemoaned the fact that in places like Fairview in the north side of Dublin, with their appalling accents, fellows played tennis in their braces and in Killester people ate cockles and, worst still, pig's knuckles. Not to mention all the kids in Kimmage! But such people never got beyond Rathmines Town Hall, so the residents of Rathgar were safe – thank heavens!

Jimmy O'Dea is remembered as Ireland's most famous comedian. In the 1920s he took part in amateur theatre productions and acted in several early Irish films produced by John MacDonagh. He then met entertainer and writer Harry O'Donovan and together they formed O'D Productions. In the late 1930s O'D Productions was brought into the Gaiety Theatre by its manager, Louis Elliman and played there until O'Dea died in January 1965. From 1940 to 1965, O'Dea also continued to tour, most notably in Australia and New Zealand in 1961, and act in films, including Walt Disney's *Darby O'Gill and the Little People* (1959).[39]

As O'Dea noted, the area was famous for the Rathgar accent and upper-class pretensions. These reinforced the view of the area. It wasn't considered Dublin, but rather 'grand' or 'West Brit'. There was also the long-standing joke about Rathgar girls, who thought 'sex' was what coalmen used to carry the coal. It originated in the 1860s, when there was a flight to areas like Rathgar, which became associated with gentility. There was even a new accent there that emphasised 'th'. The 'common' people usually referred to 'Ra'gar' or 'Ra'mines'. Many Rathgar residents looked down on Rathmines folk and their accent. They regarded Rathgar as far more exclusive. So it was not just Sean O'Casey who took issue with the Rathmines accent.

This perception among the common folk was not surprising as many of the residents were from the 'garrison', the Dublin Castle administration, or the Protestant Unionist ascendancy. Road, house and villa names in Rathgar commemorated the British administration in Ireland – its heroes, the royal family, military heroes and battles, and Anglo-Irish landlords. Albert Villa, Victoria Road, Grosvenor Road, Malakoff Villas, Brighton Road are just a few examples. Kenilworth Road and Square recall the romantic historical novels of Sir Walter Scott.

A DOLL'S HOUSE

Angela MacNamara made a name for herself when she became an agony aunt in the *Sunday Press* in 1963. She went on to be a highly respected popular columnist, lecturer on relationships, youth counsellor and author for many decades.

Born in 1931, she grew up on Rathgar Road in the 1930s and in later years lived on Zion Road. 'My kind of early childhood will never be seen again,' she noted in her book, *Yours Sincerely*. Her house was a large, double-fronted Victorian house on Rathgar Road. Wide granite steps led to the hall door. A slope for the pram and some steps led to the side entrance. The number 15 trams rattled up and down the road, travelling from the terminus in Terenure to Nelson's Pillar

Zion Road from Orwell Road junction, with Zion Road church steeple in the background. (Courtesy of NLI)

in the city centre. Beyond Terenure, the countryside began. Indeed MacNamara recalled going for picnics by the fields, streams and woods of Tallaght.

She also remembered hearing how the 1932 Eucharistic Congress brought great celebration, ceremony and devotion to Dublin. The country was *en fête*. It was a huge event since the vast majority of Irish people were ardent Catholics in those years. Flags fluttered and bunting danced in all the roads and streets of the city and around Rathgar.[40] MacNamara has photographs of her family home bedecked with flags.

At the garden end of her house there were French doors leading to a wrought-iron platform and steps to the garden. She recounted how her father 'ruled the roost with kind but no-nonsense strictness and discipline. My quiet and gentle mother bowed to his authority.'[41]

Her mother's role was that of mistress of the house and mother, but she had no say in the making of big decisions. She oversaw the kitchen staff, which consisted of a nanny, a cook, a houseman and – on Mondays – domestic help, who came in to do the huge wash.

The family had a 'grand back garden'. The house had been a private school before her parents bought it, so there was a tennis court surrounded by hedges. This doubled as a croquet lawn at times. At the far end there was a pavilion, which had been erected for the schoolchildren's indoor recreation and gym. It was a garden playroom for the children and it even had a fireplace for chilly days. When they were older, they played table tennis there. Outside the pavilion her father organised the construction of a play area, which consisted of a swing, seesaw and trapeze and was surrounded by fruit trees. High granite walls, beautified by creepers, shrubs and flowers, surrounded the garden. Such was their seclusion that the children never saw their neighbours from the garden.

There was also an adults' area in the garden. It had a teahouse facing a lawn of rose beds. According to MacNamara, this little area was known as 'Daddy's Grass'. There was no playing or messing there as he was proud of his roses and did not want them damaged. Summer lunch and tea were often served in the teahouse, which was connected to a bell in the kitchen so the maid could be called if anything was needed for the meal.

Looking back on those years growing up in Rathgar in the 1930s as post-Victorian years when domestic help was still easily available, she said, 'Our home was something of a hangover from the upstairs-downstairs homes of the previous generation.' This would have been typical of Rathgar at the time.[42]

6

STEEPLES, SPIRES, SERVANTS AND SYNAGOGUES

Rathgar is noteworthy for the number and variety of churches representing different Christian denominations. As the population increased in the area, the spiritual needs of the people had to be met. The expanding population and the rapid development of Rathgar in the second half of the nineteenth century greatly stimulated church-building. This was also a time of evangelical

A close-up of the impressive front of the Three Patrons' church, c.1900. (Courtesy of NLI)

Interior of the Three Patrons' church, in the early twentieth century, showing the three patron saints of Ireland. Note the pulpit on the left side. (Courtesy of NLI)

zeal and competition between the Christian Churches. Between 1859 and 1882, Christ Church (Presbyterian), Zion Road church (Church of Ireland), Grosvenor Road church (Baptist), Brighton Road Methodist church (1874) and Three Patrons' church (Catholic) were all built. In addition, there are a number of other, smaller churches in the area, including one for Jehovah's Witnesses on Wesley Road and a Moravians house at 27 Brighton Road.

The Jewish community in Rathgar has a fine synagogue at 7 Leicester Avenue. One of the entrance gate pillars bears the letters 'DJPC' (Dublin Jewish Progressive Congregation). The foundation stone was laid in 1952 and a façade was added in recent years. Prominent members of the Leicester Avenue congregation over the years have included the Solomon, Abrahamson and Wein families, who played a significant role in the medical, business, academic and musical life of Dublin. There is a much larger synagogue in nearby Terenure.

THE STORY OF THE PRESBYTERIAN CHURCH

The prominent and centrally located Presbyterian church (Christ Church) was built on an important site facing the village of Rathgar. The eye-catching tower is elegant in its proportions; it was designed in the fourteenth-century French Gothic style, using rustic granite masonry.

Revd Henry Cooke, DD, LLD, of Belfast, laid the foundation stone of Christ Church Rathgar on 19 July 1860. (Courtesy of Christ Church, Rathgar)

Christ Church, Rathgar, in the snow, 2010. (Courtesy of Christ Church Presbyterian Church/Caroline)

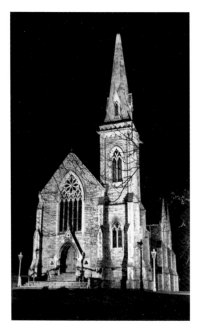

Rathgar Presbyterian church by night. (Courtesy of GCI)

A drawing of Christ Church, Rathgar, by Elizabeth Chalmers. (Courtesy of Presbyterian Church/ Elizabeth Chalmers)

Christmas in Rathgar outside Christ Church Presbyterian church, early twenty-first century. (Courtesy of Rathgar village)

Above and below: Rathgar from the air. (Courtesy of Rathgar Presbyterian church)

Presbyterians have been an influential part of Dublin's population since the early 1600s. At the turn of the nineteenth century, Dublin had a total population of close to a quarter of a million people. This figure was slowly but steadily increasing. As the population grew in size, open suburban areas such as Rathgar began to look more attractive. The more prosperous were the first to move to new houses and villas in newly developed districts like Rathgar. With the move of Presbyterian families to Rathgar plans were initiated in 1859 to build a place of worship. Several sites were inspected, including one on Rathgar Road – Murphy's Field, later the site for the Catholic church. The present site was decided upon and purchased by the end of the year.[43] It was agreed that the Scottish architect, David Heiton (of the coal merchant family), should design the new building, which provided a challenge considering the sloping nature of the site. It was decided to have the parish hall beneath the main area of worship and the church was designed in the English Gothic style of the early fourteenth century. The new church, called Christ Church, was officially opened in 1862.[44]

THE SERVANTS' CHURCH – CHURCH OF THE THREE PATRONS

With the opening-up of Rathgar from the 1840s onwards and the rapidly increasing population, it soon became clear that Catholics in the area would need a place of worship. The granting of Catholic Emancipation in 1829 stimulated a spate of church-building throughout Ireland and Rathgar benefited from this development. Many of these churches were built with an emphasis on grandeur, scale, dignity, beauty and utility. The priest who initiated the building of Rathgar church, Fr William Meagher, had been responsible for the impressive Rathmines Catholic church, which opened in 1856.

The Church of the Three Patrons was built following the donation of £2,000 by a wealthy Catholic parishioner (despite the area being predominantly Protestant and Unionist there were prosperous Catholics living in Rathgar as can be see from the wall plaques within the church dedicated to benefactors with addresses such as Fairfield House, Highfield, Kenilworth, and Rathgar and Grosvenor Roads).[45] Despite this, it was widely known as 'the servants' church' given the thousands of domestic servants that lived in Rathgar and would be able to avail of the church. These servants also contributed financially to the building of the church. Before the building of the new church the servants of the area attended Mass in Rathmines Catholic church. However, they had a propensity to continue on into Dublin city centre after the service

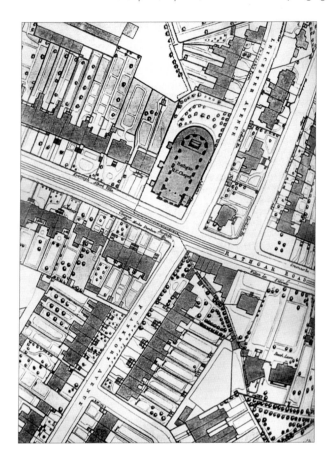

Part of a map showing
the location of the
new Church of
Three Patrons.

and the attractions (or distractions) which enticed them there. This was to
the disadvantage of the Protestant residents of Rathgar, so they preferred the
servants to have their place of worship nearer their place of work – in Rathgar.

The architect chosen to build the church was Patrick Byrne (1783–1864),
who was well known for the many churches he designed throughout Ireland.
The church was dedicated to the three patron saints of Ireland – St Patrick,
St Bridget and St Columba – on 18 May 1862, the day of its official opening,
initially as a chapel of ease for Rathmines. However, it took nearly another
twenty years to create the fine structure we have today. A pillared portico had
been part of the plans, but this was never built.[46]

That a Catholic church should be built in a mainly Protestant area of
Dublin caused something of a sensation in the newspapers of the day,
which is indicative of the social stratification and sectarianism at the time.
On 20 March 1860, *The Irish Times* warned:

On Sunday last, the Protestant and quiet township of Rathgar was the scene of mob-fanaticism and priestly display. A Chapel, it seems, is to depreciate the value of the property of the neighbourhood, and drive the Protestant occupants from the place. On the common highway, Popery was dominant and, careless of the law, marched her procession and performed her showy ritual without disguise, to the accompaniment of music and singing.

The article also described the priest's sermon as 'inflammatory and controversial'.[47]

The church was built in the Classical style. Some argue that the front of the church looks somewhat unfinished and that the exterior should have had a portico to relieve some of the severity. The façade as built was designed by W.H. Byrne in 1891. The interior has a large central space dominated by a giant order of Corinthian pilasters. Architect Jeremy Williams noted that the 'black calp exterior with its fortress of an apse has a certain rugged power'.[48]

The interior has, however, a wealth of rich architecture and religious art. The apse has an ambulatory, an unusual feature, which has tiny curved chapels with ornate shrines set into the walls. These were decorated by O'Neill & Byrne and emphasise detail and elaborate design. The first altar was a temporary wooden structure; there was no sacristy or baptistery. Eventually a handsome Carrara marble altar was erected (designed by the renowned Farrell sculptors), together with marble pavement, a balustrade and three side altars. Over the decades that followed its construction, many improvements and embellishments were added to the church to enhance it. The distinctive bronze sanctuary lamps were designed to tell the story of Moses and the burning bush. The stained-glass windows, the Stations of the Cross and the many paintings also draw one's attention, as do the baptistery with its ornate font and the mortuary chapel with its mosaic depicting the Crucifixion.

The site at 50 Rathgar Road, beside the church, later became the new presbytery and the official residence for the parish priest. Societies and con-fraternities soon followed, such as the St Vincent de Paul Society and the St Caecilian Society, which aimed to encourage liturgical music. The late nineteenth-century devotional revolution was reflected by the number and variety of devotional and novena practices, the elaborate processions, the number of sodalities and confraternities, and the number of societies that developed in the parish. By 1883 the works on the church were completed and in October of that year Cardinal McCabe presided over a major celebration.

There have been many famous persons associated with the church. One of the leaders of the 1916 Rising, Thomas MacDonagh, was married to Muriel Gifford (a Protestant) in the old tin church at Ranelagh and the story goes that at this quiet mixed wedding the witness was supposed to be Pádraig Pearse, his best friend in whose school (St Enda's) he taught. However, in the end, Pearse could not attend and consequently some other witness had to be found – and quickly. Luckily there was a man outside the church trimming the hedge who agreed to fill in for Pádraig Pearse. Four years later, in 1912, at the christening of his son Donagh in the Church of the Three Patrons, Rathgar, Pearse coincidentally happened to be in the church saying a few prayers. MacDonagh spotted him and walked up to him smiling. 'Well,' he said, 'you got here in time for the christening anyway!'[49]

STOCKBROKERS' GOLD – ZION ROAD CHURCH

Zion Road church on the corner of Bushy Park Road and Zion Road is a thriving Church of Ireland community. The building of the church owed much to the support of a Dublin stockbroker, John Goold. It opened in 1861. It has been said that Goold had been deeply moved by the inadequacy of some of the Church's responses to the spiritual and physical needs of the poor destitute people who came in droves to the outskirts of Dublin in search of food and shelter during the

Making a delivery to a house outside Zion Road church, early twentieth century. (Courtesy of NLI)

Zion Road church and school, 1861. (Courtesy of Archiseek)

famine times of the late 1840s. He initially wanted some structure or institution to be able to dispense temporal relief but opted for a church and school instead, hoping that the church would fulfil his hopes. Consequently in his will, dated 21 November 1853, he left a substantial portion of his wealth for the purchase of land on the south side of the city of Dublin for the erection and endowment of a church. Mr Goold had no relatives. He died two years later and is buried in Mount Jerome cemetery.[50]

The present site was purchase in 1859 from the Osprey Estate and two years later the church opened. The name 'Zion' was stipulated by Goold. It has nineteenth-century evangelical/Old Testament connotations and has nothing to do with the Jewish community in the area. The church was designed by the architect Joseph Welland, who adopted the Gothic Revival medieval style and cruciform plan. With attractive features, such as the miniature round tower at one end and the spire at the other, it is quite an ornate church and is further enhanced inside by stained-glass windows, an impressive organ and a carved wooden altar. It is built of granite and limestone. The *Irish Builder* magazine reported: 'these buildings, recently completed, in the rising and populous district of Rathgar, from funds bequeathed by the late John Goold, is one of the best specimens of ecclesiastical architecture as yet reared in our city or suburbs'.[51]

An interesting development in the building of the new church saw the opening-up of a new road leading to Rathfarnham – Bushy Park Road.

GROSVENOR ROAD BAPTIST CHURCH

Built in 1859 by the architects Carmichael and Jones, this fine grey structure with its pinnacled facade on Grosvenor Road is an interesting example of Gothic Revival architecture. The main entrance to the church has a fine arrangement of arches, with an attractive towering façade. Standing on the corner of Grosvenor Road and Grosvenor Place, the church is attributed to the renowned architect Edward Henry Carson and was built by English Baptists as a Baptist church for the area. It was used for some time by the Plymouth Brethren but became a place of worship for the Baptist community again in 1942.[52]

BRIGHTON ROAD METHODIST CHURCH

The Rathgar Methodist church has been serving the community in the area since 1874. It has been described as a charming example of suburban religious architecture. Located prominently on the corner of Brighton Road and Square, this simple Gothic Revival church, with its short spire, was designed by Thomas Holbrook. Further building was completed in 1879; this included work on the church, a manse and a schoolhouse. In 1924, the jubilee anniversary of its foundation, the church was extended by the erection of transepts as a memorial to the congregation's First World War dead. The school, which allowed for up to 200 pupils, was built at the rear of the church and was accessible from both Brighton Road and Garville Avenue.[53]

7

THE HIGH FIELD – DIFFERENT HOUSES FOR DIFFERENT ERAS

The part of the road from Upper Rathmines Road to Roundtown (Terenure) was built in 1753 and originally known as Cross Avenue. It was built as a link between Upper Rathmines and Rathgar. Until then Rathgar would only

The corner of Highfield Road and Orwell Road in Rathgar village. (Courtesy of GCI)

An imposing two-storey over garden-level Victorian family home brimming with character and superbly positioned with unparalleled convenience close to Christ Church Rathgar on Highfield Road, c.1850. (Courtesy of GCI)

have been approached from Dublin from Harold's Cross on up the lane later known as Rathgar Avenue. With the building of the new Rathgar Road from 1815 onwards, Cross Avenue was termed 'Old Rathgar Road' or the 'old road'. The present Highfield Road name was adopted in 1863 but Highfield appeared on maps as early as 1846 as the name of a terrace of houses, now numbers 32 to 36. It is remarkable that the numbering of Highfield Road dates from 1880, some fifty years before Terenure Road East.

It is likely that the name Highfield originated as the name of one of the fields of the original medieval farm. The original name 'High Field' is still visible on one of the pillars adjacent to no. 37. It is likely that the name Rathgar (from the Gaelic meaning 'rough ringfort') is derived from the ringfort that was located in the vicinity of Villiers and Templemore roads, just off Highfield Road.

The desire of the expanding and prospering middle classes to have properties separate from their workplaces and outside the canal boundaries resulted in house-building gathering apace on Highfield Road in the early 1860s. Until then there were only a few houses on the road. Today, the road contains a variety of houses reflecting different building eras, styles and needs. The road is attractive from the point of view of the range, type and age of dwellings, some of which are very ornate indeed. The porches of nos 13 and 14 are outstanding. The Mexican embassy's building at no. 22 is an equally impressive building. The older houses between the church and Fairfield Park are also characterful.

Rathgar House, later Oakland(s), and presently St Luke's Hospital, at no. 25, dates from around 1780, although the present rebuilt structure dates from 1853. Peachmount, at no. 51, dates from 1838 and Mountain View (no. 31) was built in 1845. Number 40 Highfield Road is a Victorian build dating from between 1842 and 1850. Ardevan House at 38 Highfield Road dates from 1846, as does Georgeville, at no. 16. Hillcourt (no. 30) dates from 1855, although it is now part of an apartment block. Albert Ville, at no. 14, dates from 1886, Alfonso from 1918 and Ardeevin (no. 71) from 1864. Fairfield House (no. 7a Fairfield Park, now no. 58 Highfield Road), dates from 1846. The newer houses alongside no. 75 date from 1927.

The impressive entrance to a Highfield Road house, a detached Victorian two-storey over basement Protected Structure of red brick over a granite base, constructed around 1885 as one of a pair. It is typical of some of the houses built in Rathgar in the late nineteenth century. (Courtesy of CODA)

The impressive mansion Highfield House at no. 37, with its two gated entrances, was built in 1848. It was the home of Richard Atkinson, tabinet and poplin manufacturer to the Queen, with premises at College Green. He lived at Highfield House from 1848 to 1868. He was also Lord Mayor of Dublin in 1857 and 1861. An old plaque, carved into one of the pillars in the mid-1800s, states 'High Field Terrace' and gives some idea of the vintage of the road.[54]

ASHGROVE AND ARDAGH

Ashgrove House near the Highfield Road corner with Dartry Road, beside the Ardagh Hotel dates from the late 1830s. The ivy-covered and yew-tree-framed Ashgrove Lodge on the corner, dates from the same time, although it looks much older, not having had the major refurbishment in recent years as its

A typical mid-Victorian villa in Rathgar. This one on Garville Avenue. (Courtesy of SherryFitz)

namesake next door. These two dwellings constitute 1a and 1b Highfield Road. The former Highfield Hotel, at 1 Highfield Road, is now the Ardagh House Hotel. The name was changed because of the confusion with the Highfield House name further along the road. Before that it was a private hotel named Clondillure. The present structure was built in 1898. The current owners deliberately chose the name 'Ardagh' to match the name 'Highfield'; 'Ardagh' comes from the Irish words '*ard*', meaning 'high', and '*atha*', field.

THE STRINGER TOUCH

In the early years of the twentieth century, house-building continued along Highfield Road. One of Dublin's most successful Edwardian builders, Thomas Stringer, put the finishing touches to his newly built houses in 1908. These fine red-bricks were somewhat different and smaller than the houses across the road, which were big Victorian two-storey structures with basements, many of them detached. Stringer's houses were built for Dublin's expanding middle classes and they were made to suit a more modern lifestyle that might not include servants, and so included gas and electrical fittings for cooking, heating and water-heating. These modern developments lightened housework considerably, lessening the need for basement kitchens and servants. These houses have four bedrooms, whereas the larger houses across the road have five. The houses would, of course, have the trademark Stringer touches, such as decorative stained glass in doors and windows, feature fireplaces and deep bay windows on both levels.

HIGHFIELD GROVE AND THE TRAMS

According to the second edition of the Ordnance Survey maps, what is now Highfield Grove, off Highfield Road, was once Tramway Terrace (locally called Tramway Cottages) – a collection of tramline cottages owned by the Dublin United Tramway Company to house its workers. Built in 1905, as the original name suggests, they were intended for the tramway workers who manned the trams or the nearby tram-yard terminus on Dartry Road. The more modern additional houses date from the 1950s.

The mostly one-storey houses were built around a green open space and although the neighbourhood has grown since those days fourteen or most of the original cottages overlooking the square are still standing today, over one hundred years later. There are even a few families that are direct descendants of the original tram workers. In the 1911 census, the average cottage in this area housed a motor man who worked for the tram company, his wife and their five children, living in approximately 560 sq. ft of space. There are also a few two-storey houses, which were built for the inspectors on the trams.

A former resident of the tramway cottages reminisced: 'I was born into one of these houses [in 1937] and they are still very much a part of the landscape. It was a beautiful place to grow up – I lived there with my family until I got married in 1961 and have the most wonderful memories of my childhood there. Palmerston Park and the River Dodder at Milltown were our haunts when we felt like wandering out of our little haven.' She recalled that when she was living in Tramway Cottages, there were sixty-five children in the twenty-five houses. Her father was a conductor on the trams.

There were many of these little enclaves of tram workers' houses in the suburbs of Dublin – the Rathgar houses were for Dartry Depot, on Dartry Road, the terminus of the number 14 tram.[55]

Highfield Grove is a unique enclave. It has a countryside feel and is remarkably quiet and unassuming.

Other roads off Highfield Road include Victoria Road and Villiers Road, which both date from 1905. Templemore Avenue dates from 1910 and Neville Road dates from 1916. Vernon Grove was built slightly later than the surrounding roads, which tend to be lined with Victorian red-bricks.

FAIRFIELD PARK

Across from Highfield Grove there is a small park in front a terrace of red-brick houses called Fairfield Park. This name derives from the attractive old house partially hidden beside the terrace: Fairfield House. Fairfield Lodge, a similarly old house on the corner with Highfield Road, begins a second terrace of red-bricks with porches in the Gothic Revival style. The terraces were constructed around the older houses in 1911.

One of the best-known residents of Fairfield (and of Rathgar) is Ulick O'Connor, barrister, writer, columnist, sportsman (a great boxer!) and renowned raconteur. He was born in the family home in Fairfield. He studied law and spent a period of time working as a barrister before becoming a full-time writer. He has published numerous works of poetry, biography, literary history and criticism and is also well known for his skills as a broadcaster and journalist. O'Connor is an acknowledged expert on the Celtic Revival; his book about this period, *Celtic Dawn*, was published to great acclaim in 1984. He was a friend and biographer of Oliver St John Gogarty. He published the first volume of his diaries in 2003, under the subtitle *A Cavalier Irishman*.

THE ABBEY CONNECTION –
DENIS O'DEA AND SIOBHÁN MCKENNA

Among the many well-known people to have lived on Highfield Road are the husband-and-wife team Denis O'Dea (1905–1978) and Siobhán McKenna (1923–1986), who lived at no. 40 (a house dating from the 1840s). O'Dea was a stage and film actor, born in Dublin. When he was a young child, he and his mother Kathleen moved in with her sister, who kept a boarding house at 54 South Richmond Street, Portobello. Denis was, like many actors of his generation, an ardent republican from his teenage years. He befriended Lady Gregory while working as a reporter in Sligo at the beginning of the War of Independence. This prompted something of a falling-out with his father Michael O'Dea, an officer in the Royal Irish Constabulary. During the Irish Civil War, Denis narrowly escaped arrest when the Free State soldier assigned to frisk him turned out to be an old school friend. Feeling the butt of O'Dea's hidden gun, the soldier quietly said, 'You had better go home now.' He worked in insurance before taking up acting. O'Dea joined the Abbey in the 1920s and became a leading member of the theatre. He was cast in a number of notable film roles, including two John Ford films in the mid-1930s, *The Informer* and *The Plough and the Stars*.

Shortly after his death, fellow thespian Gabriel Fallon recalled an encounter with former Taoiseach Seán Lemass. 'Take my advice,' Lemass counselled. 'Never play poker with Denis O'Dea. That chap plays from the cellar up!'[56]

Lemass was a regular at the poker table in the O'Dea family home at Highfield Road, which was within walking distance of his own home on Palmerston Road. O'Dea had mastered the game in the Kenyan jungles while filming *Mugambo* with Clark Gable and Grace Kelly.

O'Dea was married to actress Siobhán McKenna from 1946 until his death at the age of 73 in 1978. She was regarded as one of Ireland's

Renowned Irish actress Siobhan McKenna lived on Highfield Road, Rathgar. (Courtesy of Abbey Theatre)

greatest actors and was twice nominated for Broadway's Tony Award for Best Actress (Dramatic): in 1956 for *The Chalk Garden* and in 1958 for *The Rope Dancers*. She also acted in films, such as *Doctor Zhivago*, *King of Kings* and *Of Human Bondage*. In 1946, two years after she joined the Abbey, Siobhán married Denis O'Dea. Many consider her finest role to have been in George Bernard Shaw's *Saint Joan*. Such was her renown that she featured on the front cover of *Life* magazine. Her final stage performance was in the Druid Theatre production of *Bailegangaire* in 1985. She died the following year at the age of 63.[57]

FROM DOUBLE AGENT TO GARDA COMMISSIONER

Another well-known resident was former Garda chief Col. Eamon (Ned) Broy (1887–1972), who lived at 13 Oaklands Drive, just off Highfield Road. During the War of Independence, while a member of the Dublin Metropolitan Police (he was a clerk with the 'G' Intelligence Division from 1917 until 1921), he worked as an IRA 'double agent'. He was one of Michael Collins' three 'contacts' among the detective force in Dublin Castle and played a lead role in supplying the Volunteer headquarters with confidential reports and in

Garda Commissioner Eamon 'Ned' Broy, of the 'Broy Harriers'. Here he pulls one of the winning Irish Hospital Sweepstakes tickets in the 1940s. He had helped General Michael Collins during the Irish War of Independence. (Courtesy of GCI)

breaking the secret information system there. During this period he and his police colleague David Neligan formed the heart of Collins' intelligence service. Between 1917 and 1921, they fed him vast amounts of highly classified information and warnings. Broy was arrested by the British in February 1921 and imprisoned at Arbour Hill until the Truce. He was subsequently secretary of the then Department of Civil Aviation and later adjutant of the first Irish Air Corps, with the rank of commandant. Upon his promotion to colonel he was made Officer Commanding of the ground organisation of the corps.

In 1922 he became secretary of the Dublin Metropolitan Police and when An Garda Síochána was formed in 1925 he was appointed chief superintendent. In February 1933, he became chief of the Detective Division, succeeding Col. David Neligan. Within a month he was appointed commissioner of An Garda Síochana to replace General Eoin O'Duffy, who had been dismissed by the government. He retained that position until 1938. During his career, he established the Special Branch division, known by his opponents as the 'Broy Harriers'.[58]

WE WANT OUR COUNTRY!

Patrick Sarsfield O'Hegarty (1879–1955), who lived for many years at Highfield House, was a writer, editor, historian and a former member of the Supreme Council of the Irish Republican Brotherhood (IRB). In 1907, as Sinn Féin's London secretary, he approved and signed the membership card of Michael Collins; he later became a friend and mentor to Collins. In relation to the visit of King George V to Ireland in 1911, he famously wrote: 'Damn your concessions, England: we want our country!' He was secretary of the Department of Posts and Telegraphs from 1922 to 1945 and was elected a member of the Irish Academy of Letters in 1954.[59]

Erksine Hamilton Childers, TD, government minister and later President of Ireland, lived at 68 Highfield Road for thirty years until his death in 1922. He is reputed to have removed the main fireplace from the house to give the house a 'rural' or 'Gaeltacht' feel.

8

RATHGAR AVENUE, GARVILLE AND THE GREEK REVIVAL

Our journey along Rathgar Avenue, the oldest road in Rathgar, begins at the Harold's Cross end. The avenue, dating from medieval times, was originally a lane leading off the ancient road (*Slighe Chualann*) that connected the medieval city of Dublin to Wicklow and the rest of Leinster. The lane connected the nuns' convent at College Green with their farm at Highfield. It then went on to Rathgar Castle and the mill for grinding grain on the River Dodder. Rocque's map of Dublin from the mid-eighteenth century describes the mill as 'Lord Chief Justice's Mill'. The mill is remembered in a tiny housing enclave called Mill Close, adjacent to Orwell Bridge. Rathgar Avenue was described by the historian Nicholas Donnelly in 1908 as 'a quiet but beautiful country lane'. It still retains some of that rural atmosphere and appeal.[60]

It is a winding road, the opposite of the uniform and planned Rathgar Road, which was built in the early nineteenth century. Like Highfield Road, the avenue contains an eclectic mixture of houses, villas and cottages, reflecting many phases of building over the centuries. Converted dwellings with names such as The Stables and Coach House at the back of what was originally the stables for 31 Kenilworth Square help retain the rustic feel of the avenue, an effect enhanced by the fact that they retain the old exterior grey blocks. This is reinforced by the late nineteenth-century cottage-style houses just off the road on Brighton Avenue. Some of the old brickwork from long-forgotten times can still be seen on some dwellings, e.g. the terrace of houses at nos 4 to 8, adjacent to Harrison Row. Some of the original, surviving houses on Rathgar Avenue (particularly the cottage-type dwellings, nos 31–33, opposite Murphy & Gunn's Garage, which itself was built on the site of an old house) were built in the 1830s and lend much character to the avenue. Fern Lodge, at no. 31, is said to have been built in 1864. Number 32 still retains the old loft entrance over the former stable, now a garage entrance. Oats and hay were kept here as fodder.

The detached Eagle Lodge at 36 Rathgar Avenue was constructed in 1849. This is a prominent villa covered in unpainted stucco. In true Victorian style, the basement is set mostly above ground level. A flight of steps sweeps up to the entrance, each step narrower than the last, lending it an elegant appearance compounded by the curving wrought-iron side railings. A former coach house at the side of the house reinforces the pedigree. Number 37, Autumnville, dates from 1855, but was demolished in the late twentieth century and a small cluster of houses called Rathgar Villas was built in the back garden. Further along Rathgar Avenue, Rose Cottage dates from 1853. Evanston Cottage, at no. 60, dates from 1864. The terrace of four houses, nos 18 to 21, contains some of the oldest houses on the road. An old, blackened plaque on the wall of no. 21 has 'Rathgar Avenue' printed on it. It is an unusual location for such a sign as it is halfway along the road. This demonstrates the vintage of the terrace.[61]

GARVILLE LANE

To one side of Murphy & Gunn's garage, facing the terrace of the old cottages on Rathgar Avenue, is Garville Lane, a long and winding lane of converted mews dwellings, which were originally part of the back gardens of the houses on Garville Avenue and Kenilworth Square. The picturesque houses have original brickwork or modern variations of the old brickwork, thus staying in keeping with the tone and appearance of the original structures. The variety, style and colour of the various properties make it a particularly attractive spot.

GARVILLE AVENUE AND JACK LYNCH

It has been said that Garville Avenue is one of those roads that epitomises all that is best about genteel Rathgar. Garville Avenue links Rathgar Road to Brighton Road and crosses Rathgar Avenue. House-building on Garville Avenue commenced in 1838 and on Garville Road in the 1840s. Peterburgh, at 1 Garville Avenue, dates from 1846. Number 24 was built in 1850; railed granite steps lead to its reception hall, where ceiling cornices and ornate architraves abound. There is a variety of dwellings on this road, including villas, lodges, Victorian red-bricks and recently built houses. 'Albert Terrace' is proclaimed boldly above the terrace of houses 32 to 38. In the back garden of no. 16 there is a Second World War beehive-shaped concrete bomb shelter. These were built in many of the well-to-do properties in the area following the dropping of bombs in the Terenure and South Circular Road areas (and of course at the North Strand) in 1941. Nearby, builders found a well in a back garden of a house that was being renovated. The old well seems to pre-date the houses.

Number 21 was the home of Ireland's former Taoiseach, the pipe-smoking Jack Lynch. The Victorian two-storey red-brick was built in around 1863–6. It is a handsome two-storey house set well back from the road, behind cast-iron railings and gates. Many still recall the little wooden security hut at the entrance gate.

Lynch bought the period residence shortly after his marriage to Máirín, who was from Garville Road, for just £2,500 in 1952, when he was 34 years old, four years after becoming a TD for Cork City and having retired from Gaelic sports. The newly married couple called the house 'Lisieux'. The barrister and civil servant had previously played in eight All-Ireland finals, winning six medals in a row. Elected as a TD in 1948, he was Taoiseach on two occasions for a total of nine years in the 1960s and 1970s. It was he who brought Ireland into the European Economic Community (EEC).

For a time, Rathgar and the surrounding area was a popular haunt for government ministers and Taoisigh, with Seán Lemass, Garrett FitzGerald, George Colley, Des O'Malley and Gemma Hussey all living a stone's throw from one another. Jack Lynch died in 1999 and Máirín Lynch in 2004. The couple had lived in their Rathgar home for nearly fifty years.

Another interesting house on Garville Avenue is the unusually named Glyndwr at no. 33. It is a well-proportioned, detached, villa-style, five-bedroom house with an impressive rear garden. Built in 1845, it is one of

Ireland's Taoiseach Jack Lynch lived at Garville Avenue, Rathgar. (Courtesy of FF)

three matching houses on the road. They were constructed just before the Victorian building boom took off in Rathgar, when demand from the emerging Protestant middle class for comfortable but grand homes within easy reach of the city centre led to the development of large, two-storey-over-basement houses on the newly laid-out roads, including Garville Avenue. The builder of 33 Garville Avenue, however, looked back to a more formal Georgian style when planning the house. It is a perfectly proportioned villas, with four large rooms at hall level, four matching rooms below. It would also once have had a small scullery. The house stands on a third of an acre of land, as is the case for certain other houses in Rathgar.

RATHGAR NATIONAL SCHOOL

By the time Rathgar National School on Rathgar Avenue was built at the end of the nineteenth century, there were already many privately run schools catering for every possible need of the inhabitants of Rathgar. In 1840–41, Mrs Murphy had a seminary for young ladies on Rathgar Avenue. In 1845 Mrs Lloyd opened a ladies seminary at 1 Garville Road and the following year

Junior school boys in the late 1950s, High School, Rathgar. (Courtesy of High School, Rathgar)

Mrs Harman established her seminary at 5 Auburn Villas. This was typical throughout Rathgar until well into the twentieth century; there were a number of private seminaries, academies, preparatory and elementary schools, high schools for girls, schools for languages, mathematics and classical studies, and ladies' schools. Miss Fanny Spear was active in education for over twenty years, from 1886; David Tinkler was a 'University Grinder' operating from 57 Rathgar Avenue; and the Misses Semple were involved with the Rathgar Ladies School for many years.[62]

The picturesque low red-brick building on Rathgar Avenue is Rathgar National School and is a co-educational primary school under the patronage of the Methodist Church, who have a church at the corner of Brighton Road. The plot of ground for the school was purchased from the Hamilton family who owned much land in the vicinity of the new school.[63]

There had been a small school at the back of the church, but at the end of the nineteenth century the Methodists decided a larger structure was required and so in 1896 the Rathgar National Schools were built on Rathgar Avenue. The structure was designed as two separate schools: one for the boys and one for the girls, each with their own separate entrances. The school opened in August 1896 with 160 pupils. The school catered for mostly middle-class families that lived locally. Children of civil servants, clerks, journalists, commercial travellers, architects, teachers, clothiers, printers, accountants and merchants were well represented on the roll records.

Years later a former pupil of the school recalled a science experiment conducted by the class. A piece of bread was put in a test tube; alcohol was then poured into the tube and it was sealed. Another piece of bread was put in a test tube with water. When they were opened later on in the week, the bread in the alcohol was hard as a rock and the bread in water was still soft. Lesson learnt – they knew then what alcohol does to your food! Shortly after this the pupils were asked to take the pledge to abstain from alcohol for life.

Some of the teachers' nicknames have survived: Miss Woodcock was known as 'Cocker' and Mr Corscadden was called 'Curser' because of a certain habit of his. Memories of the old schooldays include the smell of wet clothes drying in the cloakroom by the stove (children walked to school); the fun in the yard on a frosty day when water and a brush could turn the icy ground into a slide; the shop beside the school, which sold bullseyes, aniseed drops, lengths of liquorice and lucky fizz bags; the whistling of the Bird Flanagan as he walk down Rathgar Avenue; and the games of marbles played on the way to school. Spud guns were popular with the boys, as were spinning tops and conkers. There was also a cane shop in the village where teachers bought canes for punishing students, which was standard practice at the time. For years there was a sign on a dividing wall between classrooms stating, 'Kill that Fly'! Miniature bottles of milk were distributed daily.[64]

In 1971 the schools amalgamated and became co-educational. Today Rathgar National School remains a vibrant part of the local community, as it has been for 120 years.

GEORGE RUSSELL AND THE DUBLIN LITERARY SCENE

Across from the school there is a plaque on the wall of 17 Rathgar Avenue that states:

> Poet, painter, economist, mystic
> George Russell
> Lived in this house 1911–1933
> AE

George William Russell (1867–1935), who wrote under the pseudonym Æ (signifying the lifelong quest of man), was a poet, painter, journalist and mystic. He was at the centre of the Irish Literary Revival of the late 1800s and a supporter of nationalist politics. He was born in Lurgan, County Armagh in 1867. In 1878, his family moved to Dublin, where he attended a local school in Rathmines. He grew up at Grosvenor Square. He later attended the Metropolitan School of Art, where he formed a lifelong friendship with William Butler Yeats. He came to mysticism early on and many of his poems reflect this interest.[65]

In 1897 he became assistant secretary of the Irish Agricultural Organisation Society (IAOS), which had been established in 1894 by Horace Plunkett. As a representative of the IAOS, he travelled extensively throughout Ireland, setting up co-operative banks. Though his position in the IAOS prohibited him from expressing political opinions, it was no secret that he was a nationalist. During the 1913 Lockout, he wrote an open letter to *The Irish Times* criticising the employers' actions.

At the turn of the twentieth century, Rathgar was a favoured location for the literary and political sets. Russell's house at 17 Rathgar Avenue became an important meeting place for those concerned with the economic and artistic future of Ireland. He encouraged young writers, introducing them to useful contacts and acting as nursemaid to the literary renaissance of

George Russell, who lived at 17 Rathgar Avenue for many years until 1932. (Courtesy of GCI)

Nobel Prize Winner for Literature, W.B. Yeats, was educated at the High School in his younger years. In later years his close friend, Maud Gonne, lived at Coulson Avenue, Rathgar. (Courtesy of GCI)

the time. In 1902 he met a young James Joyce and introduced him to many prominent Irish writers of the day, including Yeats. He appears as a character in the 'Scylla and Charybdis' episode of Joyce's *Ulysses*, in which he dismisses Stephen's theories on Shakespeare. Russell was a significant figure in Irish cultural life from the 1890s until the 1930s. From 1898, he and his wife Violet held 'at-homes' at their houses on Mountpleasant Avenue, 25 Coulson Avenue and later at their final home at 17 Rathgar Avenue, where he lived from 1906 until 1933. His front room was his studio and his paintings were on display here. His library at the back of the house was where he held court and imparted his wisdom to those who sat on uncomfortable chairs, ate cherry cake and listened to his discourse.

Russell was the editor of several newspapers affiliated with the IAOS, including the *Irish Homestead* (1905–23) and the leading and influential literary journal the *Irish Statesmen* (1923–30). Throughout his time with the IAOS he continued to write and publish poetry, essays, plays and novels. He also continued to draw and paint.

After the death of his wife in 1932, he moved from Rathgar to Bournemouth, England. He died there on 17 July 1935. Interestingly, one of the people at his deathbed was Mary Travers (along with Oliver St John Gogarty and Con Curran), the author of *Mary Poppins*. He had published some of her poetry in earlier years and they had maintained a lifelong friendship. He is buried in Mount Jerome cemetery, Harold's Cross, Dublin.[66]

ROYALTY AND THE BATTLE OF COULSON AVENUE

Before moving around the corner to Rathgar Avenue, George Russell lived for a time at 25 Coulson Avenue. This cul-de-sac dates from 1885 and consists of a mixture of split-level and two-storey red-brick properties built in late Victorian and Edwardian times. Maud Gonne (1866–1953), a freedom-fighting suffragette and a contemporary of Countess Markievicz, lived next door at no. 26 in the early years of the twentieth century. A well-off daughter of the garrison, it was the evictions in County Mayo in the 1880s that converted her to Irish nationalism. She founded Inghinidhe na hÉireann (Daughters of Erin) in 1900 and the organisation became influential in nationalist activities. She was the inspiration for W.B. Yeats' love poetry. Yeats wrote *Cathleen ni Houlihan* (the incarnation of Ireland) for Maud Gonne and asked her to play the part of Cathleen, which she did in 1902. She was subsequently regarded as representative of this vision of Ireland.[67]

BRIDE WHO TURNED REBEL.

Countess Markievicz, the rebel, and her husband,
who is fighting with the Russian Army, photographed on their wedding day. The death sentence
on the Countess, who is Irish, has been commuted

Countess Constance Markievicz on her
wedding day in 1901. Two years later
the couple moved to No. 1 Frankfort
Avenue, Rathgar. (Courtesy of GCI)

Maud Gonne: Ireland's Joan of Arc or 'Rebel
Queen'. Maud lived at 26 Coulson Avenue at
beginning of the twentieth century. (Courtesy
of GCI)

Some of the older residents of Coulson Avenue still recall the story of Maud
Gonne hanging a pair of her black bloomers outside her window at Coulson
Avenue during King Edward VII's visit to Dublin in 1903, ostensibly in tribute
to a recently deceased pope. She was trying to provoke her many royalist
neighbours. She succeeded in creating uproar and the police were summoned
when an apoplectic neighbour saw her underwear blowing gently in the
breeze. Her supporters arrived and tried to impede her arrest. The Rathgar
stand-off became known as the Battle of Coulson Avenue (or the Battle of
the Black Bloomers).

Loyalty to the English monarch was evidenced by the name of the small
terrace across the road from Coulson Avenue: Victoria Villas, formerly Clarke's
Cottages, a terrace of two villas dating from 1916. Further along from these
villas is Victoria Village, a gated community from the late twentieth century.

WINTON AVENUE AND THE GREEK REVIVAL

Beside the school across the road from Coulson Avenue is Winton Avenue, which connects Rathgar Avenue with Rathgar Road. The corner house on Rathgar Avenue/Winton Avenue has 'T.C. 1895' inscribed over the entrance. This avenue dates from 1864. Winton Villa, at no. 1, dates from 1866. It was described by the architect Jeremy Williams as 'the most elegant Greek Revival residential development in the southern suburbs'. Designed by Edmund Figgis, the 1860s the houses have great character and make Winton Avenue one of the prettiest roads in Rathgar. The tree-lined avenue has eight detached villas with central Ionic porticos approached by flights of steps. Five of the villas have columns, which add greatly to the grandeur of the entrances. The villas, with their period features, have the charm and grace of bygone days. On the opposite side of the road, there are a couple of semi-detached villas and a terrace of red-brick houses, all of which were built at a later stage. As is the case with many of the hidden villa enclaves in Rathgar, there is a sense of space and style on this attractive road.[68]

Greek Revival villa on Winton Avenue. (Courtesy of GCI)

AIRFIELD ROAD – HOTBED OF REBELLION AND INTRIGUE

Airfield House at 3 Rathgar Avenue dates from 1866. Nearby, on the corner with Harrison Row, was the home of Colonel James Doyle, director of the Defence Forces School of Music and the highly regarded army bands. The house was demolished in recent years, having been the subject of much controversy after planning permission was granted for new apartments on the site. For a number of years there was a gate separating Harrison Row from Rathgar Avenue, a not-unusual feature in the area.

Close by is Airfield Road, a cul-de-sac of terraced Edwardian red-bricks dating from the early twentieth century. High up on the gable end of the house on the corner of Airfield Road and Rathgar Avenue, beside the ornate street lamp, are the carved words 'JEHOVAH – JIREH'. This means, 'God will provide'. It is said that the Jewish residents of the house had it carved into the wall in the 1940s after a prayerful promise to do so should particular favours be granted.

Speech from the Dock

By F. SHEEHY SKEFFINGTON

.. ON ..

the occasion of his Trial under the Defence of the Realm Act.

" A MAGNIFICENT DEFENCE OF FREE SPEECH."

PRICE ONE PENNY.

Francis Sheehy Skeffington lived in Rathgar. (Courtesy of GCI)

Frank and
Hannah Sheehy
Skeffington lived
at Airfield Road,
Rathgar.

Always the
campaigner,
Hannah Sheehy
is on the right
of picture.
(Courtesy of GCI)

Margaret Pearse and Hannah Sheehy Skeffington, widow of the murdered Francis Skeffington, at the gates of UCD, Earlsfort Terrace. (Courtesy of NAI)

Francis and Hannah Sheehy Skeffington lived at 8 Airfield Road shortly after the houses were built, from 1903 until 1908. The couple, who were the first owners of the house, is commemorated with a plaque on the wall that states: 'Francis and Hannah Sheehy Skeffington, Feminists, Pacifists, Socialists, Nationalists, lived here 1903–1908'.

Inside, the Victorian atmosphere is palpable as subsequent owners have acknowledged the house's significance and refrained from making any major changes. One can almost hear the echoes of old, heated conversations between the Skeffingtons and their frequent visitors on the important issues of the early twentieth century. They later moved to 11 Grosvenor Place nearby. Francis was walking to this house when he was arrested in 1916. He was shot without trial in Cathgal Brugha Barracks, Rathmines.

Johanna Mary (Hannah) Sheehy Skeffington, (1877–1946) had, along with her husband and Margaret and James Cousins, founded the Irish Women's Franchise League in 1908 with the aim of obtaining women's voting rights. She was later a founding member of the Irish Women's Workers' Union.[69]

EGGS, BUTTER AND BOMBS

There was also much animated conversation across the road from no. 8, at no. 16, for it was here that Michael Collins, one of the leaders of the War of Independence, often covertly stayed with friends, the O'Donovans, who were bankers from Cork. The O'Donovans had a dairy shop (now Rathgar Travel) on Rathgar Road. The family later moved to 10 Garville Avenue. But in the meantime Michael Collins found a safe haven at no. 16, regularly having Sunday dinner and sometimes hiding out there for weeks at a time. He was there around the time of the Bloody Sunday massacre in Croke Park in November 1920 and it was in this house that Collins had many important meetings with Dublin and Cork leaders of the struggle for Independence. The house was also used as a depot for the delivery of guns, which arrived concealed in egg cases and bombs in butter cases. Michael Collins also used a flat on Grosvenor Road when in Dublin.[70]

Other well-known residents of Airfield Road included the actor, Des Perry, renowned for his portrayal of Jack Nolan in *Tolka Row*. This was a hugely popular soap opera in the 1960s and was set in Dublin's north side. It was based on the play of the same name written by Maura Laverty.

The renowned pianist Charles Lynch (1906–1984) also lived on Airfield Road. He was once described by Arnold Bax as 'Ireland's most imaginative pianist' and was regarded as the country's premier concert pianist for many years.[71]

FROM BIRD-STUFFER TO NOVELIST – WILLIAM CARLETON

William Carleton (1794–1869), a popular nineteenth-century novelist and writer, spent most of his working life in Dublin, notably at 1 Rathgar Avenue, now incorporated into Comans Pub premises. The old brickwork of his house can be seen on the back wall of the pub.

Carleton was best known for his *Traits and Stories of the Irish Peasantry* (1830), a collection of ethnic sketches of the stereotypical Irishman. Born in County Tyrone, Carleton's father was a Catholic tenant farmer who supported fourteen children on as many acres. Young Carleton spent his early life witnessing scenes similar to those he later described in his books. Carleton was steeped in folklore from an early age. His father, who had an extraordinary memory (he knew the Bible by heart) and was a native Irish speaker, had a thorough acquaintance with Irish folklore and often told stories by the fireside. His mother, a noted singer, sang in the Irish language. Carleton received a basic education.

The headstone, in Mount Jerome cemetery, of William Carleton of No. 1 Rathgar Avenue. (Courtesy of William CarletonSociety/fotofinish)

Rathgar village with
Comans on left. The former
Munster & Leinster
Bank is beside the pub.
(Courtesy of GCI)

William Carleton,
a nineteenth-century
novelist who lived
at No. 1 Rathgar
Avenue for many years.
(Courtesy of GCI)

THE WORKS

OF

WILLIAM CARLETON.

VOLUME III.

TRAITS AND STORIES OF THE IRISH PEASANTRY:

NED M'KEOWN.	THE HEDGE SCHOOL.
THE THREE TASKS.	THE MIDNIGHT MASS.
SHANE FADH'S WEDDING.	THE DONAGH; OR, THE HORSE STEALERS.
LARRY M'FARLAND'S WAKE.	PHIL PURCEL, THE PIG-DRIVER.
THE BATTLE OF THE FACTIONS.	THE GEOGRAPHY OF AN IRISH OATH.
THE STATION.	THE LIANHAN SHEE.
THE PARTY FIGHT AND FUNERAL.	GOING TO MAYNOOTH.
THE LOUGH DERG PILGRIM.	PHELIM O'TOOLE'S COURTSHIP.

THE POOR SCHOLAR.

THE BLACK PROPHET.

WILD GOOSE LODGE.

TUBBER DERG.

NEAL MALONE.

ART MAGUIRE.

ILLUSTRATED.

NEW YORK·

P. F. COLLIER, PUBLISHER.

1881.

Traits and Stories of the Irish Peasantry by William Carleton. (Courtesy of GCI)

Illustration from Traits and Stories of the Irish Peasantry by William Carleton. (Courtesy of GCI)

" HOW HE KEPT HIS HATE SO LONG HAS PUZZLED ME FROM THAT DAY TO THIS. "—*Shane Fadh's Wedding,* p. 685, *l. and S. of the I. P.*

Illustration from *Traits and Stories of the Irish Peasantry* by William Carleton. (Courtesy of GCI)

'The Hedge School' from *Traits and Stories of the Irish Peasantry*.

As his father moved from one small farm to another, he attended various 'hedge' (outdoor) schools, which used to be a notable feature of Irish life. A picture of one of these schools can be found in the sketch entitled 'The Hedge School' in *Traits and Stories of the Irish Peasantry*.

Carleton sought a job as a bird-stuffer to start his working life. However, his proposal to use potatoes and meal as stuffing failed to impress his prospective employer. He then tried to become a soldier, but the colonel of the regiment dissuaded him; Carleton had applied in Latin. After staying in a number of cheap lodgings, he eventually found a place in a house in The Liberties, on Francis Street, which contained a circulating library. The landlady allowed him to read for twelve to sixteen hours a day. In 1830 he published his first full-length book, *Traits and Stories of the Irish Peasantry* (2 vols), which made his name and is considered his greatest achievement. In it he stereotyped the Irish 'Paddy' in sketches such as 'Phil Purcel the Pig Driver'. He was, in his own words, the 'historian of their habits and manners, their feelings, their prejudices, their superstitions and their crimes' (preface to *Tales of Ireland*). He moved to Rathgar Avenue in 1854. He died in 1869 and is buried in Mount Jerome cemetery.[72]

9

RATHGAR ROAD AND VILLADOM

Rathgar Road is the polar opposite to Rathgar Avenue in many respects. It is nearly a mile long and is very straight and uniform. It dates from *c.* 1815, when it was constructed to link Rathmines with Highfield Road and Roundtown Road (Terenure Road East) at the Rathgar village junction and then on in the direction of Rathfarnham Road.

For some years the road remained without a single dwelling to 'relieve its monotonous straightness or interrupt the view of the open pastoral country through which it passed', according to the historian, Weston St John Joyce, in his *Neighbourhood of Dublin*. It was first shown on Taylor's 1816 map as 'New Road', without any houses. It continued to be known by later Rathgar

Some of the impressive houses on Rathgar Road. (Courtesy of GCI)

Typical entrance to a Rathgar house. (Courtesy of GCI)

residents as 'the new road' until the early twentieth century. Highfield Road was known as 'the old road'. When it was being built, at the section where it met the upper end of Highfield Road, now the village, there stood a few thatched cottages and an inn, the latter a favourite hostelry for country people going in and out of town by that route. This group of houses became known as 'The Thatch' and was known by that name for many generations of people living in the outlying parts of south County Dublin.[73]

Rathgar was an exclusively rural district until the 1840s, when a few detached residences began to appear. Some of the oldest properties date from the 1830s or 1840s, including the villas at Auburn Villas and Belleville Avenue. Early houses were in the Georgian style and dwellings in Rathgar are noted for their richly decorated features, excellent plasterwork and joinery.

In his book *Victorian Dublin Revealed*, local resident Michael Barry noted that the *Dublin Builder* rhapsodised about Rathgar Road in 1859 that 'villas, single and semi-detached, terraces etc., are springing up with an almost fairy-like rapidity' and 'the green sward speedily gives way to macadamised roads with populous thoroughfares'.[74] However, what we see today as a straight, uniform road did not come to be so all at once. Like most of Rathgar, it was built villa by villa or terrace by terrace. There were times when building gathered apace, particularly in the 1860s and 1870s.

The styles of building reflected the social position and ambitions of the middle- and upper-class, mainly Protestant, households that took root in Rathgar. The early residents of Rathgar Road were generally senior civil servants of every hue, members of the professional, employer and managerial classes, with a high proportion of domestic servants, whereas the residents of Brighton Square, slightly farther from the city, were lesser officials from a wide variety of backgrounds. James Joyce's father, a commercial traveller and somewhat impecunious, would have fitted into this category when his son was born there in 1882. According to Mary Daly in her work on Dublin's Victorian houses, 'Protestant and Unionist Dublin middle-class could evade the unpleasant reality that they were a minority which was increasing losing political control in both Ireland and in the city of Dublin'.[75]

The housing stock on the new road developed gradually over the succeeding decades, gathering momentum in the 1860s. Today there is still evidence of the names of successive terraces and their numbering, which was introduced in 1866.

Thomas Grant and family pictured in 1910. He was a superintendent in the Dublin Mounted Police (DMP) and was based in the Rathmines/Rathgar area. The family lived at 24 Rathgar Road. (Courtesy of the Grant family)

Typical interior of a house on any of the principal roads in Rathgar. (Courtesy of GCI)

The ornate ceiling of a Rathgar house. (Courtesy of GCI)

Early houses were built of brick and fitted with Georgian sash windows. The door-case pillars of the Georgian houses were retained in some cases in later changes but many were replaced with wood-panelled pilasters/columns with carved brackets. Many Victorian architects were fond of opulently decorated pilasters, which can still be observed on some doorways and windows on Rathgar Road and Terenure Road East. Richly plastered interiors, arched doorways and plain or coloured fanlights and external decorative ironwork were popular. The variety of house designs on the road and in Rathgar more widely helps to make this area so distinctive: the colouring; the decoration and styling of the brickwork (red and yellow); as well as the slating, railings, motifs, balconies, doorways and porches, windows, chimneys and eaves.[76]

VILLAS, LODGES AND HOUSES

One- and two-storey villas of the type still seen in Rathgar were popular in the middle of the nineteenth century. These grand dwellings (often smaller inside than they seem from the outside,) with their granite steps sweeping up to the entrance, reflected the owners' aspirations to be seen as similar to country gentlemen. The villas had the hint of a gentleman's country residence and were often designed to look impressive. Some of these consist of one storey over a basement. The main reception rooms were on the first floor and were approached via a flight of granite steps. The kitchen and extra space for bedrooms, etc., could be found on the ground floor. The villas were generally detached, although on Rathgar Road there are a few semi-detached villas.

Some of the houses on the road have been demolished and replaced with modern apartment blocks, particularly at the village end of Rathgar Road, near the Presbyterian church, but most are still intact. Many of the houses have retained original period embellishments and features: original gateposts and decorative railings at the front; ceiling coving and centrepieces; original cornice-work; sash windows and shutters; panelled doors and architraves; timber floors and handsome marble fireplaces.[77]

THE ELEGANCE OF PERMUTATIONS

A typical mid-Victorian terraced house would have a generous flight of steps leading up to the hall door, which would have recessed panels, solid mouldings

The sailor suits worn by little boys during the mid to late nineteenth century. The trousers in this variety were long legged and were often worn with a wide-brimmed straw hat. James Joyce himself was photographed as a young boy wearing a sailor suit. (Courtesy of Orla Fitzpatrick/ Jacolette/Wordpress)

Blouse and skirt combinations were very popular during the 1890s and 1900s – this would have been the fashion for young ladies of Rathgar. (Courtesy of Orla Fitzpatrick/ Jacolete/Wordpress)

A teenage girl from Rathgar holding a dome-top birdcage at the close of the nineteenth century. (Courtesy of Orla Fitzpatrick/Jacolette/ Wordpress)

and decorative support pillars. They typically also had a rendered façade and Victorian sash windows, often with ornate surrounds. Decorative brickwork was often a feature, as were decorated cast-iron railings for the steps and the front gardens, an abundance of chimneys (as houses had at least one fire lit every day of the year for cooking purposes), and stained glass in some windows (often in the fanlight over the entrance). Interior decoration included ornate plasterwork in halls and main rooms, impressive and often elaborate marble fireplaces with large mirrors over them in the drawing/sitting room, ceiling roses and cornices, mahogany handrails on the banisters, and William Morris floor tiles, which were popular at the time.[78]

In *Victorian Dublin Revealed*, Michael Barry notes the corbelling (brick projecting from the wall) of some of the red-brick houses, a technique that reflects the Victorian elegance of Rathgar. This is evident in abundance on

A Rathgar teenager in late nineteenth century holding a tennis racket. Tennis was becoming increasingly popular as evidenced by the opening of the Brookfield and Ashbrook LTC's early in the twentieth century. (Courtesy of Orla Fitzpatrick/Jacolette/Wordpress)

Rathgar Road and the surrounding area. Elegant villas in a simple classical style are hallmarked with such features as a cast-iron detail over the entrance or cast-iron detailing on the door or surrounds in what Barry calls 'a bewildering array of permutations'. One unusual addition is the moulded horse's head on the wall beside the entrance of no. 46 or the large eagle on the edge of the roof and over the entrance of no. 30.[79]

CASTLES, COACHES AND CRIMEA

Another of the many distinctive houses on Rathgar Road is Castle Cottage, hidden away at No. 103. This white-fronted house is more a small castle than a cottage, with its wrought-iron battlements and towers, its impressive front door and its large front garden. The present structure was most likely built on an earlier cottage that serviced Rathgar Castle. When the new Rathgar Road was built, the cottage (later Castle Cottage) and the adjacent terrace of four dwellings, Roseaire Villas, were back from the road and so they were hidden away when new houses were built fronting the road. As a result, it is difficult to appreciate Castle

Cottage (or the villas), except by walking down a gated laneway to view them. The cottage is important structure architecturally, historically and geographically and it was a vital part of the early development of Rathgar village.

Of particular interest also are the few surviving coach house entrances/ gates to be seen along Rathgar Road. These would have been used by prosperous residents for their own horses and carriages, which were kept in stables behind the houses. Most other residents walked to work or used the trams and servants from the tenements either lived in or walked. So these coach-house entrances belonged to well-to-do families who were able to pay for a mews for the horse and carriage and accommodation for the groom. There is an impressive, small cluster of them with distinctive large and high gates still intact beside the houses along the road (nos 143, 145, 146 and 147 in particular), nearly opposite the Three Patrons' church.

The house at 185 Rathgar Road, called Malakoff House, is a striking semi-detached Victorian residence. Next door, no. 184, is called Malakoff Villa.

Malakoff House. A striking semi-detached Victorian residence on Rathgar Road. The name commemorates a battle of the Crimean War. (Courtesy of GCI)

The house derived its name and style from the Crimean War (1853–56); both houses have urns or trophy-like edge-of-roof decorations as well as crouching lions over the first-floor windows. Victorian Dublin had many memorials to those who participated in the numerous wars fought by the British Empire around the globe. The Crimean War made a big impact. Malakoff House and the nearby Alma House on Grosvenor Road were both named after the war. The two Malakoff houses were named after the battle at the Malakoff bastion at Sevastopol, which was a Russian fortress. After the fall of the fortress to the Allies (including Britain), peace was possible. These houses were built in the late 1850s.[80]

NUMBERS OF TERRACES

For many years houses and villas were known by their names. It was not until Rathgar Road was completely lined with houses that numbers started to be used. The use of terrace names for clusters of houses also preceded the numbering of houses, which was introduced in 1866.

The development of housing on the road can be appreciated when one considers the names of houses, with their dates and their present number-ing: Surrey Lodge, 175 Rathgar Road, 1834; Melrose Villa, 176 Rathgar Road, 1834; Roseair Villas (terrace of four), 98–101, 1838 (originally called Sarzey and renamed in 1851); Mullach Ban, 114, 1840s; Beechlawn, 158, 1846, although the date 1829 has also been mentioned; Rathgar Cottage, 124, 1840s; Salisbury Villa, 149, 1849 (now called Ballagh); Ellerslie, 157, 1850; Valentia Lodge, 21, 1860; Weston, 26, 1862; Brumelia, 156, 1864; Kingston Lodge, 24, 1864; Ontario Lodge, 23, 1864; Richmond House, 30, 1864; Lucretia, 22, 1877; Winton 25, 23, 1900; Wilton Lodge, 156, c. 1900; and St Joseph's (Legion of Mary), 191, 1910.

Some terrace names still survive, but quite a few have seen the houses demolished for redevelopment purposes. A case in point is Spire View, now replaced by a road with modern houses built in the late twentieth century. Each decade from the 1830s to the 1860s saw the construction of a new terrace, e.g. 1833, Spire View at nos 31 to 43; 1834, Melrose Villa at no. 176 and in 1838, Sarzey (renamed Roseair in 1851) at nos 98 to 101; 1843, Belleville at nos 132 to 137; 1850s (late), Grosvenor Terrace at nos 44 to 46; 1850s (late), Malakoff Terrace at nos 184 to 187; and in 1864, Stanley Terrace at nos 181 to 183.[81]

FACES AND PLACES

Many famous people lived on Rathgar Road. Someone of importance lived in practically every house along this road and the adjoining roads of Rathgar at some time in the history of the area. The detached villa, Mullach Ban at 114 Rathgar Road, was home to some of the Andrews, a family with a political dynasty. The family is said to have played a part in inviting John F. Kennedy to Ireland in 1963 as the Andrews had close connections with the Kennedy family.

Number 53 is associated with the 1916 Rising. On the eve of the Rising, an important meeting took place in this house, organised by Eoin MacNeill, who was chief-of-staff of the Irish Volunteers (but not the IRB). He counter-manded the order for the Rising to go ahead at Easter. He was a good friend of Dr Séamus O'Ceallaigh, an obstetrician, who owned the house. Unsure of the wisdom of going ahead with a rebellion, MacNeill called a meeting at the house. The house was often visited by some of those in national-ist circles and those involved in organising the Rising, including Arthur Griffith, The O'Rahilly, Thomas MacDonagh, Seán T. O'Ceallaigh and others. Messengers were sent to different parts of the country with the message that Rising had been cancelled. It was said there never was a plot or conspiracy attended by more noise or less concealment. The meeting resulted in much confusion and severely reduced the number of Volunteers that reported for duty on the day of the Rising, since Pearse, Connolly and others all agreed that the Rising should go ahead. It began on Easter Monday, 24 April. Dr O'Ceallaigh later recalled that the atmosphere in the house was 'surreal' because of all the well-known personalities in attendance.[82]

Interestingly, the house was located in very heart of the largest concen-tration of Protestant Unionists outside what later became Northern Ireland. The president of the Loyal Orange Lodge, Dublin Branch, lived around the corner in Kenilworth Square and a chief superintendent based in Dublin Castle lived at 24 Rathgar Road. Some of the participants fighting for the 10th Batallion Royal Dublin Fusilliers during the Rising had family or relations in the Rathgar area. However, this unusual situation was a feature of Rathgar and Rathmines prior to and after the Rising, with staunch Nationalists living side by side with Unionists. One of the leaders of the Rising, Thomas MacDonagh, a Catholic, married Muriel Gifford, who came from a staunch Unionist family from the Palmerston Road area. Another leader, Joseph Mary Plunkett, married her sister, Grace Gifford. Moreover, Ernest Blythe, born in Ulster of staunch Protestant Unionist stock, fought in the War of Independence and later became an Irish government minister. He lived in Kenilworth Square.

From left to right: W.T. Cosgrave, Ernest Blythe (who lived at Kenilworth Square for many years), Kevin O'Higgins and James J. Walsh. (Courtesy NAI)

In the 1940s, during the Emergency, the residents of Rathgar Road witnessed a shoot-out between the Gardaí and IRA activists in a shop premises at no. 99a. This was a time when Éamon De Valera's government was cracking down heavily on the movement. Two detectives from Dublin Castle, Gardaí Richard Hyland and Patrick McKeown, were among five Gardaí searching the house on 16 August 1940 when they were showered with gunfire from behind a partitioned wall. Hyland died instantly. McKeown died the following day.

John O'Leary, the old Fenian immortalised in W.B. Yeat's poetry, lived at 134 Rathgar Road in 1889. The following year, he moved around the corner to 39 Grosvenor Road.

Thomas Corless, the owner of the famous Dolphin Hotel, just off Parliament Street, and the Burlington Dining Rooms at Oyster House, near Dame Street, lived on Rathgar Road in the 1880s.

Joseph Kirk, the renowned sculptor, lived at 60 Rathgar Road in the 1860s. He was well known for his portrait busts. However, many consider his lasting legacy to be his production of the spectacular Siege of Seringapatam in India on the Wellington Monument in Dublin's Phoenix Park. The monument itself commemorates the successes of the Irish-born Arthur Wellesley, the first Duke of Wellington, at the Battle of Waterloo and elsewhere. Kirk also created the impressive Crampton memorial. He is buried in Mount Jerome cemetery and his grave, near the Victorian chapel, is adorned with an impressive monument.

Dr George Little moved to Weston at 28 Rathgar Road in 1930. As well as being a doctor he is remembered for his historical writings, particularly *Dublin Before the Vikings*. He was president of the Old Dublin Society from 1942 to 1955 and was largely responsible for the opening of the Dublin Civic Museum in 1953.[83]

Advertisement for the Dolphin Hotel in 1913. While not on a par with hotels such as the Metropole and the Shelbourne, which in 1913 boasted passenger lifts, electric lighting and even fire escapes, the Dolphin was a very popular hotel and many Rathgar residents frequented it. The restaurant was one of the best in the city with good value: 2s 6d and 3s 6d table d'hote dinners. Other popular restaurants in Dublin in 1913 were Mitchells, Bewleys and Jammets.

The demolition of the Crampton memorial, 1959. The memorial, at the junction of College Street with Pearse Street and D'Olier Street, was erected from the design of John Kirk in 1862. It consisted of a bust above a fountain surmounted by a cascade of metal foliage. The monument was locally known as the 'water-babe', and later as the 'cauliflower', 'pineapple' or 'artichoke'. As it was slowly falling apart, it was removed in 1959. (Courtesy of Irish Press/MC's Fotofinish)

Number 47 Rathgar Road, a large and distinguished-looking detached house on the corner of Leicester Avenue and Grosvenor Road, has in recent years been listed as a 'Protected Structure'. This is thanks to the sterling work of the Rathgar Residents' Association. For years this was an abandoned and derelict dwelling, an eyesore for residents and travellers alike. In ten years of campaigning, this house has been the subject of two planning battles, ongoing enforcement battles and a suspicious death investigation following the discovery of the body of a Ukrainian girl on the property. Now, however, the house is rising from the ashes again and has returned to its former glory, all the while adding considerably to the beauty and distinctiveness of this part of Rathgar.

FRANKFORT AVENUE

Rathgar Road is intersected with some fine roads, including Frankfort Avenue and Leicester Avenue beside the Three Patrons' church. Some houses on Frankfort Avenue date from 1843 but most were constructed from

The wedding of George and Susan Ebrill 1905 at University Church Stephen's Green. The family lived at various times at 68 Frankfort Avenue and 58 Grosvenor Road. Susan Ebrill lived at Grosvenor Road until her death in 1930. He was Professor of Chemistry at the Royal University of Ireland, subsequently called the NUI (National University of Ireland). (Courtesy of the Humphrys family)

1864 onwards. Number 1 is a large, low and distinctive house with long narrow windows. It is dwarfed by its neighbours, yet the originality of its design make it as a landmark building on the road. It is also of historical importance.

Constance Markievicz (*née* Gore-Booth) (1868–1927) married a Polish count she had met in Paris. In 1901 they came to live at St Mary's, 1 Frankfort Avenue. The house was a wedding present from her mother. Nearly on the corner, it is still one of the more distinctive houses on the road. (It later became the presbytery for the nearby church.) Seemingly, the newly married were not too popular with their neighbours, who disapproved of gardening on Sundays, amongst other activities. In 1909 Markievicz moved from St Mary's to 9 St Edward's Terrace, Rathgar. She fought in the 1916 Rising with the Irish Citizen Army. She was second in command to Michael Mallin at the Royal College of Surgeons. After being arrested, she was court-martialled and sentenced to death, but the sentence was commuted because of her gender. Between 1916 and 1924 she endured five long terms of imprisonment. In the general election of 1918, while she was a prisoner in Holloway, she was elected to the British House of Commons. This was the first time a woman had been elected.

Another prominent resident of Frankfort Avenue was George Du Noyer (1817–1869), a geologist and artist who lived in a house called Dunloe in the 1860s. He studied art under George Petrie and worked with the Irish Ordnance Survey as a draughtsman. The Royal Irish Academy has eleven volumes of his drawings.

The Ebrill family outside 58 Grosvenor Road in the 1930s. (Courtesy of the Humphrys family)

Susan Ebrill and her children, 1919. (Courtesy of the Humphrys family)

The name Leo Maguire will ring a bell for people who listened to the Walton's Music-sponsored radio programme on Radio Éireann in the 1960s and 1970s. This was a popular programme, promoting the famous Walton's music shop on the corner of Parnell Street and North Frederick Street in Dublin. Maguire used to finish with the line, 'If you sing a song, sing an Irish song'. He lived at no. 47 for many years.

Clarendon House, Terenure Road East. (Courtesy of Sherry Fitzgerald)

The family of Cornelius Ryan, author of the book *The Longest Day* (subsequently made into a major film), lived at no. 35. He had previously lived in Portobello.

As is the case all over Rathgar, the coal holes on the avenue are individually designed for each house. Likewise, the lamp posts are distinctive.[84]

LEICESTER AVENUE

Leicester Avenue connects Rathgar Road to Kenilworth Square and some of the houses date from 1845. The Disneyesque – or, as one resident described it, the 'gingerbread and Victoriana type' – house, Leicester Lodge, at no. 8, was built in 1846 (possibly as a Dower House). One of its former residents was the renowned military historian, General Hogan. The houses at St Patrick's Terrace on Leicester Avenue were built in 1860. Lark Vale, at no. 7, dates from 1860 and Invermay House (no. 6) was built in 1892. Interestingly, the small back gardens of a few of the houses on Grosvenor Road (e.g. no. 29) have exits onto Leicester Road and are given separate numbers from the houses. There is a good view of the back and side of the Three Patrons church (with the three 'blind windows'), in particular the fine bell tower, which has

'A.D. 1906' carved beneath the bell. There is also an entrance to the back of the Queen of Peace Nursing Home to allow residents to access the church.

BELLVILLE AND AUBURN

Rathmines Park dates from 1865. Rathgar Place is a lane between no. 171 and no. 172 Rathgar Road. The old exposed grey limestone brickwork on the side wall of no. 172 is noteworthy as one can see some of the ingredients of house-building in the mid-nineteenth century. The long lane walls are still standing and lead to converted mews dwellings at the rear of some of the Rathgar Road houses.

Farther along Rathgar Road, Belleville Avenue has three impressive Regency-style single-storey villa residences that date from 1838 to 1847. These villas have some character and although they are detached, having been built over the course of a decade, they look like an attractively uniform terrace when viewed from a short distance. They turn this near cul-de-sac into another of the many hidden gems in Rathgar.

Albany and Cranford are tree-shrouded enclaves containing a couple of mid-Victorian villas beyond Belleville and just off the Rathgar Road. Close by is the almost hidden entrance marked Auburn Villas. Auburn Villas is a mature, picturesque, residential L-shaped terrace, which enjoys a great seclusion and tranquillity. It is a cul-de-sac containing a small collection of genteel Victorian houses. The handsome façade of Primrose Cottage, a superb Regency gem dating from 1834, immediately catches one's attention. Some

Partial front elevation of AIB Bank in Rathgar village, constructed around the 1920s.

of the other bigger houses are also attractive. Auburn House is hidden away behind one of the villas. Nearby is 158 Rathgar Road, a one-storey villa built in the front garden of an older villa to the rear.

Wesley Road dates from 1915 and Winton Avenue dates from 1864.

TERENURE ROAD EAST

Continuing on from Rathgar Road and through the village junction we have Terenure Road East, formerly called Roundtown Road or Upper Rathgar Road. The boundary between Terenure and Rathgar is at Ferrard Road on one side, beside the old road marker that states 'From G.P.O. 3 Miles', and beside the old cottage on the opposite side, where a bollard has the 1847 inscription of the Rathmines and Rathgar Township on it. So from Rathgar village up to this marker is Rathgar, beyond which Terenure begins.

Terenure Road East started as a footpath across fields from Upper Rathmines Road to Terenure. It became a road early in the 1800s when the new Rathgar Road was being constructed. For a few years around 1860 it was regarded as a continuation or part of Rathgar Road. The early entries in the directories from 1834 are more specific; in them, it is called 'Rathgar Road from Roundtown'. In 1862 it became Roundtown Road. Ten years later it became Terenure Road. In the same year there were forty-eight ratepayers on the road, fifty-eight in 1872, eight-two in 1882 and ninety-four in 1892.[85]

The current designation of Terenure Road East was not adopted until about 1930. That was also the time that house numbers were introduced: until then, residents specified their address by the name of the house or terrace, as was the case in much of the rest of Rathgar.

House-building proceeded at a good rate in the important year of 1860, although Pleasantville dates from 1815, Mote View dates from 1836 and the gracious and imposing double-fronted Clarendon at no. 46 dates from around 1843. Susan Ville dates from 1846, Sylvan Lodge, at no. 73, was built in 1850, and the Victoria Terrace houses at nos 11 to 29 were built in around 1852. Cremorne (no. 71) dates from 1851. Dunlewey (no. 31) dates from 1855, as does Clevedon (no. 35), Montrose (no. 39) and Malvern (no. 37). Victoria Villa (no. 9) was built in 1856, although it was subsequently demolished in the 1920s to make way for the present AIB bank building. Tyrone House dates from 1874. Stratford House, at no. 59, dates from 1877. Glenone (no. 48) dates from 1881 and Brookline, at nos 56 to 58 dates from 1870 (a wall plaque stating this is still intact).

James Davy addressing the Irish Stock Exchange in 1944 as its president. (Courtesy of the Davy Group)

SNUFF AND STOCKBROKERS

Arguably one of the most magnificent, if not the most distinguished, houses on the road is located between Dunlewey and Clevedon (no. 33). This four-storey detached house is an eclectic villa with adjoining mews, both of which are crowned with Jacobean-style gables. It was originally called Hopeton and was built in 1861/2. It is an outstanding structure, replete with ornate details, an impressive frontage and a double-pillared granite entrance porch at the top of a flight of steps. The carved gable is an outstanding feature and is repeated in miniature on the remarkable former coach house built beside the main house. The house was built for George Mitchell, an importer of snuffs, tobacco and wine, which he sold in his shop on Sackville Street (now O'Connell Street). It also has links to the Brown Thomas families.[86]

Across the road from Hopeton is Brighton House at no. 50, on the corner with Brighton Road. It dates from 1864. Next door at nos 52 and 54 are two outstanding dwellings, Avondale and Triest, built in 1890. The intricate artwork, tiling, wrought-iron balconies, arched and ornate porches, and the French windows catch one's attention. The Gothic-style door cases and porches are attractive features. Even the eaves have prominent brackets on these ornate houses. Both houses add much to the distinction of this part of Rathgar.[87]

Other houses on the road are also prominently decorated. Glenarm and Roslin, at nos 61 and 63 respectively, just before the Rathgar boundary with Terenure, though partially hidden by old trees, are noteworthy for their beautiful brickwork and other decorative features. Number 34 is interesting also, although shabby, as it has a Roman head over its attractive doorway. Farther along towards Rathgar village, the decorative ironwork on the door panelling of some of the houses is attractive.

Number 29, near Rathgar village, was the birthplace of James and Eugene Davy, the brothers that founded the famous firm of stockbrokers of the same name. At the turn of the nineteenth century the family was associated with a number of pubs, including the J&T Davy Pub at Portobello Bridge (now the Portobello Hotel). James had been advised to go into stockbrocking by his UCD Economics professor, and, in 1926, he became a member of the Dublin Stock Exchange. He was soon joined here by his brother Eugene. They established J&E Davy, which had its first office on Westmoreland Street. The brothers built up the business over the next few decades thanks to the slowly emerging Irish middle class.

HEDGE-HOPPING IN RATHGAR

An interesting story relates to Clarendon (no. 46). The year 1934 brought triumph and tragedy in equal measure for one of the Aer Lingus founders, Colonel Charlie Russell, then residing at Clarendon. In May of that year, the former British services First World War combat pilot and two other Irish airmen wrote to the government to outline their plans for a new national airline – a blueprint which became the foundation stone of the national carrier. Thirteen years before this, Charlie Russell had become the first commanding officer of the Irish Air Corps and Michael Collins' 'getaway pilot'. Collins ordered him to go to London to purchase an aircraft prior to the 1921 Treaty negotiations. If things went wrong, Collins was to escape by air. Russell spent £2,600 on a Martinsyde biplane (christened 'The Big Fella'), which, in the end, wasn't required. The plane was shipped home nonetheless, making it the first aircraft owned by the newly independent nation.

But on 10 September of that year, Russell witnessed the death of his nephew Arthur in a plane crash right in front of his house in Rathgar.

Captain Arthur Russell, who had followed in his uncle's footsteps as a pilot, took a three-seater Irish Air Corps Fairey 111F biplane up from Baldonnell and decided to impress his uncle by 'buzzing' his house. Witnesses said the plane had been diving hard, pulling up and 'hedge-hopping'. But the captain flew too low, collided with the top of a tree opposite Clarendon and crashed into Justice Meredith's garden. Colonel Russell ventured outside just in time to see his nephew's plane explode into flames. Arthur was killed instantly, along with another passenger.[88]

10

THE WINDMILL AND THE
WASHERWOMAN – ORWELL

Orwell Road begins in the village of Rathgar and continues on to Churchtown and through Milltown golf course. It had no special name when houses were first built there in the nineteenth century. In the 1830s the residents gave their address as 'Garville' and in the 1840s and 1850s as 'Rathgar'. It was also called

The Old Wind Mill at Rathgar Quarry painted by George Petrie (1790-1866). (Courtesy of NGI/GCI)

Windmill Avenue, the name deriving from the drainage windmill at Rathgar
Quarry, which was used to power and control the levels of water in the quarry
during excavation work. This name was officially adopted in 1860, but not for
long; four years later it was changed to Orwell Road. The quarry was on the
site that is now occupied by Herzog Park. The windmill survived until the early
1900s on a bluff just beside Glengyle, now Stratford School, Zion Road.

For many years the most notable feature of the road was this large quarry
of 'black stone', the calp limestone. The quarry was in existence for generations but became more useful from 1800 to 1900. Stones for Portobello
Barracks were drawn from the quarry, as, according to tradition, were stones
for Archbishop Minot's great tower at St Patrick's Cathedral, begun in about
1372. The limestone was also used to build many of the garden walls in the
area. The quality was not good, so it was used for the walls of the basements
of houses and then plastered over. It was also used on roads. Many of the
houses in the area were built with Portland cement and later with machine-
made red bricks from brickworks, such as the nearby Mount Argus and
Dolphin's Barn brickworks.[89]

The official opening of Herzog Park, Orwell Road, in 1995.This park was opened to celebrate
the tri-millennium of Jerusalem. Included in the picture is Dublin's colourful Lord Mayor, Sean
Dublin Bay Rockall Loftus and Chaim Herzog, Prime Minister of Israel. (Courtesy of Dublin City
Council/GCI)

The Rathgar quarry had various names, including Rathgar Quarry, Rathgar Stone Co. and Jordan's Quarry, depending on who owned it. The noise from the quarry, however, was a source of annoyance for the growing population and the quarry eventually closed in around 1900.

The quarry was a picturesque location that attracted the attention of artists including George Petrie (1790–1866), who painted *Old Wind Mill at Rathgar Quarry, Dublin* (now in the National Gallery of Ireland), and William Sadler. The landscape painter Jeremiah Mulcahy ARHA lived at 2 Orwell Road in the 1870s.

Dublin Corporation took over the quarry and used it as a landfill. However, problems soon arose with the draining of the quarry as some adjacent properties were experiencing subsidence. The draining was stopped and dry filling continued instead. Eventually, Herzog Park was built on the old Rathgar Quarry site. It was officially opened in 1985 by Chaim Herzog, Prime Minister of Israel. His father had been Chief Rabbi of Ireland and lived in Portobello. The park's opening celebrated the tri-millennium of Jerusalem.[90]

WASHERWOMAN'S LANE

This was the popular name for the laneway serving the backs of the Highfield Road houses just off Orwell Road in Rathgar village. The washer-women occupied small cottages named 'Orwell Cottages' that were demolished in the early 1950s, although if one ambles up the narrow winding lane some old brickwork is still apparent.

Serious house-building started on Orwell Road in the early 1860s, although there were sporadic builds as early as the 1830s. For example, another Rathgar House, now Orwell House, was built in 1810 and Mountain View was built at 2 Orwell Road in 1838. Houses were still being built in the 1950s; Montpelier, (no. 64), was built in 1954.

CRYSTAL PALACE AT DUNFILLAN HOUSE

Travelling along Orwell Road, past Stratford Haven and Lodge, we have the Lucena Clinic run by the Hospitaller Order of St John of God at 57–59 Orwell Road. This was originally Dunfillan House, the home of wealthy Dublin businessman, David Drummond, in the nineteenth century. It was designed as a villa by Charles Geoghegan in 1865. Drummond was one of the commissioners of the Rathmines and Rathgar Township. His namesake Thomas

Drummond was the powerful and influential Under-Secretary for Ireland until his untimely death in 1840. It was he who coined the phrase 'property has its duties as well as its rights'. He is buried under one of the largest mausoleums in Mount Jerome cemetery in Dublin.

The old house still stands and is now part of the St John of God educational complex. The glass conservatory near the house is also still standing in all its glory. This is a distinctive and elegant structure, much appreciated by the Irish Georgian Society, which supported its renovation in recent years. This conservatory was referred to as a 'Gentleman's Crystal Palace'. Inspired by the popularity of glasshouses in the nineteenth century (including the ones in Glasnevin's Botanic Gardens) and his association with the Dublin Exhibition Palace and Winter Garden in Coburg Gardens, Drummond's secondary purpose for the conservatory was to create a recreational space. The structure was most likely designed by the renowned Dublin ironmonger, engineer and sculptor Richard Turner (who designed the glasshouses in Glasnevin's Botanic Gardens) or someone inspired by his work.[91]

These early cricket-related photographs show two brothers, David and John Drummond, the sons of the wealthy businessman and philanthropist David Drummond of Dunfillan House, Orwell Road, in the 1860s. Both boys are wearing quite fancy outfits which may or may not be part of their school or cricket uniforms – they attended Rathmines School. David was born in 1852 and subsequently became a renowned physician in England. (Courtesy of Orla Fitzpatrick/Jacolette/Wordpress and posted in Cricket Photographs)

FROM FAUNAGH TO MARIANELLA

The picturesque Marianella Lodge guards the entrance to Marianella, home to the Redemptorist Order for nearly 100 years. An old Victorian postbox can still be found on the external wall. Across the road a headstone-like stone, embedded in the old grey wall states, 'From GPO 2 Miles', though the lettering has faded over the years. Next to the modern building complex that is Marianella, there are a couple of acres of gardens. Overall it is an extensive plot of land, measuring approximately nine acres.

The Redemptorists originally purchased a house at 30 Highfield Road in 1910, which they named 'Marianella'. The purpose of the house was to provide a residence for Redemptorist students attending the National University of Ireland near the city centre. The new house proved to be too small, so in 1919 a larger house was purchased at 75 Orwell Road, known at the time as Faunagh House.

This had been the home of the Colley family for some years before they left Rathgar in 1916 and moved to Corkagh House, then owned by the Finlay family, in Clondalkin. The Colley family had great military connections. One ancestor

A 1909 portrait of Edith Maud Olivia, wife of George Pomeroy Arthur Colley, of Faunagh, Rathgar. (Courtesy of Laetitia Lefroy)

was the Duke of Wellington, of Waterloo fame. Another was Sir George Pomeroy Colley, a major-general in the Boer War. The writer Elizabeth Bowen was a cousin of the family. The Colleys were also connected by marriage to the Lefroys. The Lefroys are a long-established Huguenot family who came to Ireland after fleeing persecution in Flanders. There were links with the Austen family and Jane Austen was a particular favourite of the young Thomas Lefroy in the nineteenth century, when they met in Hampshire. Lefroy went on to become Lord Chief Justice of Ireland (until 1866); he sentenced some of the Young Irelanders to transportation to Van Dieman's Land (Tasmania). George Pomeroy Arthur Colley was the last of the family to live in Faunagh. He sold the house a few years after his marriage to Edith Finlay in 1908.

In the 1960s the old Marianella was demolished and a new seminary was planned for the site. The new Marianella opened in 1968. As well as housing the students and missioners, it became the home of the Provincial Administration and Redemptorist Publications, the publishing arm of the Province which publishes the well-known *Reality* magazine. In 1974 the present chapel at Marianella was opened. Around this time Orwell Road itself was widened. It had been a much narrower and more winding road. Marianella had to surrender part of its land for this purpose.

Although Marianella was the home of Redemptorist students until 2010, it became clear, as student numbers decreased, that the building was not being used to its full potential. In 2015, in the light of declining number of candidates for ordination to the priesthood, the Redemptorists decided to sell the premises and land. It changed hands for a reported €40 million.[92]

TEACHERS AND HOTELS

There are three impressive red-brick houses just past Marianella. The three villas, one of which is detached, were built in 1886 for members of the Drummond family (of Dunfillan House). They are noteworthy because of the range of decorative devices used by the architect, Charles Geoghegan: panels, arches, columns, windows, brickwork, tiles and even the chimneys are lavishly decorated.

The first of the houses, at no. 69 (later the Carrick Hall Hotel), was originally built and opened under the name Aberfoyle for W.H. Drummond of the well-known garden seed and implements shop on Dawson Street. In recent years it has reverted to a private dwelling. It was later called Carrickbrack and the house next door was called Rockdale.

The Teachers Union of Ireland occupies the third house on the terrace, no 71, and uses it as its headquarters. This is also a large and impressive two-storey late Victorian house. The stylish railings of cast- and wrought-iron fronting the property are an interesting feature due to their elaborate shapes, twists and decorations. Such remarkable railings are prominent throughout Rathgar. At the side of this house are the former stables, which overlook the front garden. They have been converted into private dwellings.[93]

The Orwell Lodge Hotel at 77a Orwell Road on the corner with Orwell Park was formerly Woodhurst, and was built in 1864. It was a nursing home before it became a hotel. It closed in the early years of the twenty-first century for renovation. Two houses were built adjacent to the former hotel on some of its land. The hotel has since been converted into apartments.

ROSTREVOR

Opposite Marianella, behind a triangular private park, is Rostrevor Terrace. One of the attractions of Rostrevor Terrace is the way the whole terrace is screened from the main road by mature trees, creating a quiet, private road of terraced two-storey over-garden-level residences, built in around 1864. Most of the fourteen houses have five or six bedrooms and three reception rooms. Rooms are rich in period detail and they have 8ft-high ceilings, intricate cornicing, white marble Italian fireplaces, sash windows with shutters and exceptional mantelpieces throughout, which lend these houses great elegant. Ornate large white urns are strategically placed on the walls in the open spaces between every two-house terrace.

From 1878 one of Dublin's most prominent businessmen, William Martin Murphy, was listed with a residential address at 7 Rostrevor Terrace, then from 1883 he was listed as having an address at the much more upmarket residence of Dartry Hall around the corner at Orwell Park. This move reflected the growth of his income and social status during this period.

Another famous resident of the terrace was the architect George Palmer Beater (1850–1928) who lived at no. 1. He was one of Dublin's most renowned and prolific architects in late Victorian and Edwardian Dublin. He specialised in commercial architecture. Beater was born in Dublin on 16 June 1850, the son of Orlando Beater, of Glenarm, Terenure Road East, chairman of the famous department store, Arnott & Co. He designed many of the fine houses in Rathgar, including some impressive dwellings in nearby Orwell Park. As well as that, he had designed Arnott's department store, which had launched his career. He also designed one of the four corner buildings at the junction of O'Connell Street and Middle Abbey Street, which later became the *Irish Press/Evening Press* offices.

He so loved Rathgar that he lived in five different homes in the area: Rostrevor Terrace, 1873–1879; St Helen's, Highfield Road, 1881–1882; Glenarm, Terenure Road East, 1883–1896; Minore, St Kevin's Park, Dartry, 1897–1922; and 9 Brighton Road, where he lived from 1923 until his death in 1928.[94]

Orwell Park house in the French chateau style. (Courtsy of GCI)

House on Orwell Park designed by George Palmer Beater. His own house, 'Minore', would have been just behind this property in St Kevin's Park, also accessed from 23 Orwell Park. (Courtesy of Savill's/fotofinish)

Rostrevor Terrace leads to Rostrevor Road. Most of the houses along this road date from 1930. This quiet cul-de-sac affords a beautiful view of the Dublin Mountains. Near its end, hidden behind a hedge, is a little enclave of old cottages built around an open area. The entrance lane to this tranquil haven is marked by a black bollard and leads to Woodbine Cottage, the former lodge of Rathgar Estate. A number of other quaint dwellings go by the name of Wilmar Cottage, Rosevale, Somerville and Newbarn. Time seems to have stood still in this small square, which is like a miniature village. An old gable wall of a barn still bears signs of a loft.

From the end of Rostrevor Road, at Ardkeen House (situated on a quarter of an acre of land), there is an impressive view of the High School's tennis courts and the trees of the Dodder River valley. This Stringer-built home positioned at the end of the picturesque cul-de-sac dates from 1927.

ORWELL HOUSE AND THE BETHANY HOME

Returning to Orwell Road from Rostrevor one comes across the Orwell Lodge Nursing Home, perched on the edge of the Dodder River Valley. It was formerly Orwell House and in the early decades of the twentieth century, it was a Protestant orphanage known as a Bethany Home. A Bethany Home was founded in Blackhall Place in Dublin in 1921; it moved to Orwell Road in 1934, where it was based until it was closed in 1972.[95]

The present complex consists of the old Orwell House, which was built in the 1830s (although some claim an earlier date of 1810) and retains many of its period characteristics. Attached to this is a three-storey modern extension, which contains most of the bedroom accommodation. It was originally called Rathgar House (there were three Rathgar House dwellings in Rathgar at one time) and built by the businessman Patrick Waldron, who owned a linen drapers company and who operated a calico printing works overlooking the nearby River Dodder. In 1852, *Thom's Directory* stated: 'Near the Dodder, until very lately, there were calico printing works, of Messrs. Waldron, worked by steam and water-wheel power, and giving employment to a great number of persons.' The house and factory were subsequently owned by a William Carvill, who operated a sawmill there. The house changed hands a number of times since until it came to be owned by the Walker family. Joseph Walker was a dentist.

The Bethany Home that was located in this house was not a Magdalene laundry; it was a refuge/detention centre for 'fallen' Protestant women and unmarried mothers. It also cared for their children and children who became orphaned if their mothers were imprisoned by the courts for prostitution and lesser crimes. Some of the former residents claimed many years later that children were mistreated in the home and suffered an unusual level of ill health. In 2010, 219 unmarked graves of Bethany babies and children were discovered in Mount Jerome cemetery in Harold's Cross.[96]

The name of the house was changed to Oak House when the Girls' Friendly Society took it over as a hostel in 1973. It later became a nursing home.

Behind the nursing home, bricked off by an old grey barn wall, is the timeless enclave, accessed via Rostrevor Road, containing the original Orwell House lodge and some cottages.

The weir on the River Dodder below Orwell Bridge, c. 1881. In the background are the former Waldron's Calico Print Works, later Rathgar Sawmills. (Courtesy of GCI)

Further down the steeply sloping Orwell Road is a dwelling called The Barn at no. 114d. This dates from 1937. Across the road is a house, appropriately called Highview, perched with its stepped garden on the edge of the river valley. It would appear that this part of Orwell Road was cut out of the steep banks of the River Dodder many years ago to create a bridge over the river. The Kiosk, at Orwell (originally Waldron's) Bridge, has been the source of much happiness for children playing in Dodder Park since the 1940s. Across the road is Mill Close, a tiny enclave of houses that serves as a reminder that the old Waldron calico mills were located nearby.

ABERCROMBIE AND DODDER

The River Dodder was one of the major industrial rivers of Ireland for many years and is still dotted with many mill wheels, weirs, sluices and old factories. It was also one of the main sources for the drinking water of Dublin.

The river stretches for 18 miles, from its source high on Kippure, which is the highest mountain in the Dublin Hills at 757m, to where it enters the Irish Sea at the three great locks of the Grand Canal in Ringsend. For most of its course, the Dodder is a beautiful line of green, a linear park which owes its existence to a Scottish town planner by the name of Abercrombie. In 1941 he was commissioned by the County Borough of Dublin to examine possible

Parent and child gazing into to River Dodder, near Ely's Arch, in 1957. (Courtesy of GCI)

Postcard showing the banks of the River Dodder in early the early twentieth century. (Courtesy of GC1 Images)

uses. Among many other recommendations, he proposed that the Dodder River Valley should become a public amenity. While Abercrombie's vision has never been fully implemented, you can still walk or cycle the Dodder in either direction between Firhouse and Ringsend; there is a path the whole way, with just a few road-crossings to join up the sections. Along the way you might see the remains of the old sluice-keeper's cottage at Dartry Park.

In contrast to the neighbouring areas of Harold's Cross (park opened in 1890s) and Dartry (Palmerston Park also opened in 1890s), there was no public park in Rathgar until the 1930s. Dr Lombard Murphy presented a stretch of the grounds of Dartry Hall on Orwell Park that adjoins and overlooks the River Dodder to the Dublin Corporation. The linear park along the Dodder was extended when the Corporation bought the lands originally used as the drying grounds of the nearby calico-printing factory. This also included the ruins of a limekiln, which, to the delight of generations of children, is still standing near Ely's Arch, a former entrance to Rathfarnham Castle. Residents of Rathgar are fortunate to have such a wonderful amenity on their doorstep.[97]

HURRICANE CHARLIE

Many residents of Rathgar will remember when eight inches of rain that fell on Kippure Mountain poured down into the River Dodder and combined with four more inches of rain that fell on the city in 1986 because of Hurricane Charlie. The river burst its banks and there was widespread flooding in Rathgar and elsewhere along the route of the river. Orwell Gardens, near the bridge, was badly affected.

Beside Orwell Bridge, we have Orwell Walk and Dodder Vale, a long picturesque road, overlooking the river and the weir and guarded by weeping willows. For many years there was a cottage practically on the weir. The residents were employed by the nearby mill to open and close the sluice gates to regulate the flow of water to the turbines in the mill.

Parts of the Dodder near Rathgar are popular for fishing and angling. The fishing season starts on 17 March, St Patrick's Day, and runs until the end of September. Trout, eel, salmon, stone loach and three-spined stickle-back may all be found in the river. There is also a life-sized rhino to be found in the river, albeit a bronze one, which appeared overnight in 2002 and can be seen from the bridge beside the Dropping Well Pub.[98]

THE EMBASSY BELT AND THE BOTTLE TOWER

Beyond Orwell Bridge, on the opposite side of the Dodder River valley, is Mount Carmel Hospital, which overlooks the surrounding area. Past the small enclave of newish pale-coloured houses, called Landore, is Thorncliffe Park, which was built in the mid-1940s on the land of the old Thorncliffe House. One of the entrance pillars to the estate still stands. The Russian Embassy opposite was formerly the headquarters of the Irish Management Institute (IMI), before which it was home to the Kinahan family, who were wholesale fruit merchants with shops on O'Connell Street and Westmoreland Street. Eaton Brae, beside the embassy, is interesting as it is the site of a large and striking old house, Ard na Greine, which dominates the road. On the opposite side of Orwell Road is Stirling Park, where there is an old, grand house, now renovated. Some of its land has been used as a site for the building of expensive houses, which are hidden behind a tree-lined driveway.

The small number of houses on nearby Green Park were built around an old renovated house called Dundarave. Building commenced in the early 1930s when one of Dublin's busiest builders, John Kenny, offered buyers a choice of eight styles of house on the nine-acre plot. He promised in his brochure that 'no effort will be spared to see that the houses are well-built, bright, homely and healthy'. He intended building many more houses in the cul-de-sac, but buyers bought multiple plots in order to have large gardens, with the result that there are now just ten houses. Like Stirling Park, this is an exclusive enclave of magnificent manses built around a circular area filled with mature trees. These houses, like so many in Rathgar, have everything – location, scale, character, large gardens and beautiful, ornate façades. One of the houses is on a third of an acre of mature garden and was once owned by former well-known publican Ned Finnegan, owner of the Bottle Tower pub in Churchtown and Larry Murphy's pub on Baggot Street. For many years he lived in this five-bedroom detached house. The enclave is surrounded on one side by Milltown golf course and the twelve-acre Russian embassy complex on the other. Like other hidden gems in Rathgar, this lends Green Park a feeling of tranquillity and seclusion. More of these fine houses can be found along Orwell Road, just before the golf course, and have the Green Park address.

Commemorative plaque for Frank Lawlor who was ambushed on Orwell Road near the Milltown golf course during the Irish Civil War. (Courtesy of NGA)

Across the road from these impressive detached houses, before the Milltown golf course, there is an old boundary marker stating, 'Co. Boro. Bdy', thus marking the old county borough boundary. Beside it there is a wall plaque, erected by the National Graves Association and written in the old Gaelic script, marking the tragic death of the IRA member Frank Lawlor, who was ambushed and murdered at that spot on 29 December 1922 during the Civil War. For many years this part of Orwell Road was known as 'ambush corner'.

THE ANGEL AND THE MONUMENT CREAMERIES

Many of the older residents in Rathgar will remember the Monument Creameries shops that were located all over Dublin, including in Rathgar village. The owner of this chain of creameries lived at Rockdale (one of big red-brick houses near Marianella) on Orwell Road. He was Séamus Ryan (1895–1933), a Fianna Fáil member of the Irish Senate (Seanad) from 1931 to 1933. He was very active in the War of Independence and used some branches of his shop as depots for republicans during the conflict. Even butter boxes were used! These had false bottoms to hide dispatches and ammunition for IRA operations. It was said that Ryan had such an innocent, angelic face that no one guessed at the subversive nature of his business.

Senator Seamus Ryan, of Fianna Fail, lived at Rockdale, Orwell Road. (Courtesy of FF)

Outside one of Seamus and Kathleen Ryan's Monument Creamery shops in 1938. (Courtesy of Archiseek)

Ryan's political career was cut short when he died suddenly at his residence in June 1933. The young senator was given a State funeral. Taoiseach Éamon de Valera and every member of his cabinet (with one exception) were in attendance. The centre of Dublin came to a standstill as the forty-vehicle cortège passed thousands of sympathisers who lined Parnell Street before it paused for two minutes outside the head offices of Monument Creameries on Camden Street. Finally the tricolour-draped coffin was carried to its resting place, just metres from the grave of O'Donovan Rossa in the Republican Plot at Glasnevin cemetery on the shoulders of his friend, Dan Breen, a parliamentary colleague and Irish revolutionary hero who was also a resident of Rathgar.[99]

TELESCOPE ON ORWELL

Howard Grubb (1844–1931) was another famous resident of Orwell Road (no. 14 and, at different times, Aberfoyle and Rockdale). On Observatory Lane, off the Rathmines Road (beside the Cricket Club), there was a remarkable telescope-making factory owned by Howard Grubb. He made not only sophisticated telescopes but also scientific instruments, periscopes and gun-sights. The company made telescopes for various governments across the world, including two for the tsarist regime in Russia just before the 1917 revolution. The telescopes were subsequently paid for by the new Bolshevik government. Grubb was also associated with the Greenwich, Armagh and Dunsink observatories. In 1887 he was knighted by Queen Victoria.[100]

ORWELL PARK

Orwell Park is one of South Dublin's most prestigious and favoured roads. It is lined with stunning, detached, red-brick-fronted, bay-windowed and all-round magnificent dwellings built for people of some importance in Dublin. In the late nineteenth and twentieth centuries, this would have consisted primarily of businessmen and professionals, but in more recent times, these have been joined by artists and musicians, e.g. Michael Colgan of the Gate Theatre and Bill Whelan of Riverdance fame (both former residents). This reflects the changing nature of Irish society and the movement of wealth to different classes.[101]

House-building on Orwell Park commenced in 1864, although Dartry House and Oakland pre-date this. However, from the 1860s and 1870s a number of large houses were built along the impressive tree-lined road. There are few houses that were built later, such as no. 15, which has '1895' carefully inscribed above the front door. The style of the houses on the road represented a new development and differed from houses on nearby Rostrevor Terrace, which were bigger in order to accommodate domestic servants and more facilities. In the houses on Orwell Park, there was no need for the full flight of steps and basement kitchens seen in some older Rathgar residences. Such houses were no longer fashionable – or necessary. The styles had changed from three- and four-storey houses to modern two-storeys.[102]

An original entrance gateway to Oakland House (now St Luke's Hospital) on Orwell Park is still in situ and is used mainly as a pedestrian entrance. It bears the decorated monogram of Charles Wisdom Hely, one of the original owners of the house. The gates are surmounted by a pair of elaborate leaf scrolls.[103]

New properties built on Orwell Park in recent years are located on a site which was formerly owned by the Mill Hill Fathers and, prior to that, by the Murphy family, whose most famous member was William Martin Murphy.

MINORE AND THE NUNS' HOUSE

Some of the houses built on Orwell Park were designed by one of Dublin's most famous and prolific Edwardian architects, George Palmer Beater, who designed two identical houses next to each other for two of his children in 1904. The houses were situated on the grounds of his own house, Minore, in St Kevin's Park, which backed on to Orwell Park and which has an entrance to this day on Orwell Park (no. 23) with the name Minore displayed.

Nearby, 28 Orwell Park is a distinctive six-bedroom detached house, but it was built much later than its Edwardian neighbour and looks a little like the religious institution it once was – the pebble-dash house with no hint of the red bricks so much a feature of most of the houses thereabouts is known locally as 'the nuns' house'. It is detached and has the attractive appearance of a small French château.

Many of these houses boast magnificent period features, including marble and cast-iron fireplaces throughout, high ceilings, fine cornicing and centre roses, working window shutters, picture and dado rails, leaded stained-glass entrance doors and windows, and much more.

Every house on Orwell Park has its own distinctive features. No two houses are alike. Some are particularly remarkable, including no. 14, Fernhurst, which is a Victorian Gothic Revival house with an adjoining conservatory. Number 58, called Lisnoe, is a detached, asymmetrical villa that was built in 1886. It is a beautiful house that stands in its own grounds. Across the road is one of the entrances to Beater's Minore and farther along on the same side is Ingleside (no. 36), a villa built in 1900, with half-timbered gables, bay windows and a verandah. Detached houses are a feature of this end of Orwell Park, each more resplendent than the next, including Kintullagh (no. 34), Rosheen (no. 36) and Mount Alvarna on the corner of Orwell Park and Dartry Road.

DRACULA AND THE PLAYBOY

Former residents of Orwell Park include Abraham Stoker Jr, better known as Bram, who was born in Marino, but spent some of his formative years at no. 5 (now no. 4) Orwell Park, from 1863 to 1868. He became known as the author of *Dracula* thirty years later. Born in the house where Bram Stoker had lived was John Millington Synge (1871–1909). His family lived there from 1871 (after the death of his father, who died of smallpox) to

1890. The family moved from Rathfarnham to the house next door, that of his maternal grandmother. He is said to have developed his lifelong love of ornithology while studying the birds along the banks of the nearby River Dodder. The High School on Zion Road has a collection of his stuffed birds.

Synge's masterpiece was *The Playboy of the Western World*, which was first performed at the Abbey Theatre in 1907 and caused riots. Five hundred policemen were required to keep order in the theatre and the nearby streets. One line from the play – 'A drift of chosen females standing in their shifts' – caused the trouble, particularly the word 'shift'. The mere mention of it provoked enormous opposition and a week of riots.[104]

11

DARTRY ROAD AND THE STEAMBOAT LADIES

Orwell Park connects to Dartry Road, which begins at the junction of Upper Rathmines Road, Highfield Road and Palmerston Park and continues beyond the former Dartry Dye Works near the River Dodder at the Dropping Well

One of first wardens of Trinity Hall outside one of the houses of residence at Dartry Road. (Courtesy of TCD)

pub. This road, although part of the separate area of Dartry, is intrinsically linked with Rathgar and the distinction between the two is blurred such that residents of both areas sometimes claim to be part of the other area. This is similar to the situation on Grosvenor Road, where some residents claim to be residents of Rathgar and some claim to be residents of Rathmines. The confusion possibly arose because Dartry Road once began at 215 Upper Rathmines Road, where there is a plaque on the front of the house that reads: 'Fitzwilliam Terrace, Lr Dartry Road, Upr Rathmines, 1905'.

Houses on Dartry Road date from around 1840s. St Kevin's House, at No. 21c, was built in 1849. Cora Linn (no. 2) was built in 1874 and nearby Santon dates from 1877, whereas Coolraine (no. 2b) dates from 1948.

STEAMBOATS AND THE BOTANIC GARDENS

Located on Dartry Road, facing the older houses, is Trinity Hall, the most important residence for students of Trinity College Dublin (TCD). There are three detached Victorian mansions in the grounds surrounded by modern red-brick halls of residence. The purpose of the new student residences, first used in the first decade of the twentieth century, was that they were to be used to accommodate female students in Trinity so that they would not be a 'danger to men' or a distraction to the male students at the Trinity campus in Dublin's city centre. It was also important that the residences should be in a nice part of Dublin and not too far from the college. The Dartry Road location was deemed most suitable for all the needs.

An unusual aspect of the history of the halls in the early decades of the twentieth century related to the 'steamboat ladies' – those Oxford and Cambridge female students who had to come to Dublin on the steamboat to be conferred with their degrees by TCD, since their own universities did not allow them to receive degrees. Under an arrangement between the three universities over 700 students travelled to Dublin, stayed at Dartry Hall and were conferred in TCD.[105]

Oldham House was the main place of residence of the college until the early 1970s. The two other buildings are called Purser and Greenane houses. Oldham House is a fine, detached Victorian building named after Elizabeth Oldham, one of the main campaigners for women's admission to the college. Her portrait hangs in the front lounge. The hall continued to be used as a residence for women until the 1970s, when the first men were admitted.

Also on the Trinity Hall grounds at Dartry is the new (since 1968) home of the centuries-old Trinity College Botanic Garden. The Botanic Gardens, connected to the botany department at Trinity, moved to a site at Trinity Hall when the lease on the original site in Ballsbridge (where the two hotels were built on the corner of Lansdowne Road) was bought back – hence some of the slightly more exotic trees in the area. There were vegetable plots there, which continued to supply the hall with produce for meals. A fresh bunch of flowers would be picked and placed in a vase in the hall of Main House each week. The gardens gradually turned more and more to experimental growing and some of the area which was mostly used for the orchard was used in the new build a decade ago.

Despite that, the gardens boast some 1,000 species of plants and more than 100 varieties of shrubs and trees. A plant with the striking name of *Crocosmia Lucifer* is patrolled regularly by a black cat, appropriately called Lucy. The name derives from the deep red colour of the flowers, which are like giant golden irises. There are also ponds, beehives and glasshouses in this haven of tranquillity, which boasts its own micro-climate.[106]

Students and warden outside Oldham House at Trinity Hall in the 1940s. (Courtesy of TCD)

DARTRY DYE WORKS AND THE QUEEN

There were a number of mills built along the River Dodder in the eighteenth and nineteenth centuries. Dartry Limited was established in 1888 as the Dublin Laundry Company, with its works beside the Nine Arches and the River Dodder at Dartry. All that remains is the free-standing towering chimney that used to be part of the works. In 1900, the laundry claimed to be the second largest in the United Kingdom and Ireland and was the official launderer to Queen Victoria when she visited Ireland in 1900. The company had several branches throughout the city and suburbs.

In 1895, an old mill near where Dartry Road slopes down to the Dodder was converted into the Dartry Dye Works. The red-brick building, known as the Counting House, was added in the 1920s. In 1955, the two businesses amalgamated under the name The Dublin Laundry and Dartry Dye Works. It ceased business in 1983 as an increasing number of homes had washing machines and had no need for laundries. Not too long afterwards, two other laundries that catered for the houses of Rathgar, the Kelso Laundry in Rathmines and the Swastika Laundry in Harold's Cross, also closed.

Dartry Laundry electric delivery van. The Dartry Laundry delivery van is on display at the National Transport Museum, Howth, County Dublin. It dates from 1946 when it was originally a bakery van for Kielys bakery and it passed to the Dublin Laundry Company of Milltown in 1950, where it remained in use until 1982. (Courtesy of Michael Corcoran)

Dublin Laundry van. Dartry Ltd was established in 1888 as the Dublin Laundry Company, with its works beside the Nine Arches and the River Dodder at Milltown just down the hill from Dartry Road. In 1900, the laundry claimed to be the second largest in the United Kingdom and was official launderer to Queen Victoria when she visited Ireland in 1900. The company had several branches throughout the city and suburbs. Dartry Laundry closed in July 1982, after ninety-four years in business. This battery-powered vehicle epitomises the era when Dublin had more than twenty-five commercial laundries. (Courtesy of Michael Corcoran)

Today, the Counting House of Dartry Dye Works is still standing, though now it is used as offices. 'Est. 1895' is carved between the still-working clock and the stained-glass windows. Under the windows the words 'Dartry Dye Works' are still emblazoned over the old front entrance of this fine red-brick building. The clock, which is now digitalised, is so popular with passers-by that when it stopped a number of years ago, the public were so disconcerted that many wrote to the owners requesting that it be fixed post-haste. The adjacent buildings, Dartry Mills, were demolished and new offices were built, although they retained the old name. A steep and winding road leads down to Dodder Park.[107]

THE *FREEMAN'S JOURNAL* AND JOHN GRAY

John Gray (1816–1875), the controversial owner of the *Freeman's Journal*, was a long-time resident of Clareville on Dartry Road. He was a doctor who was indicted for conspiracy in 1843, knighted in 1863 and served as an MP for Kilkenny from 1865 to 1875. There is a statue of him on Dublin's

Sir John Gray. He had a house in Rathgar.

Sir John Gray's grave in Dublin's Glasnevin cemetery. (Courtesy of fotofinish)

O'Connell Street to this day. The statue commemorates his involvement in bringing Vartry Reservoir water into Dublin City, particularly to Rathgar residents, for whom the water issue was a persistent problem for decades. His successor as owner of the *Freeman's Journal* (later called the *Irish Independent*) was a Rathgar neighbour, William Martin Murphy, who lived at Orwell Park beside Dartry Road.

ST KEVIN'S PARK – DIFFERENT HEROES IN DIFFERENT ERAS

Near Highfield Road, just off Dartry Road, is St Kevin's Park. The residences here date mainly from 1905 onwards. St Kevin's Park was home to a number of people with illustrious careers, including former government ministers Professor Martin O'Donoghue and Gemma Hussey. The legendary hero of the War of Independence, Dan Breen, also lived there. The latter was a Fianna Fáil politician for nearly thirty years. He lived at 9 St Kevin's Park, Dartry. During the Irish War of Independence, Breen had a £1,000 price on his head. However, he quickly established himself as a leader within the Irish

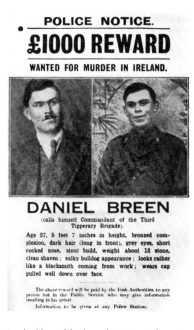

'Looks like a blacksmith'. Wanted poster of Daniel (Dan) Breen, during the Irish War of Independence. Breen lived most of his life at 9 St Kevin's Park, Dartry and was a Fianna Fail TD for over thirty years. (Courtesy of FF)

The Atom Splitter. Nobel Prize Winner, Ernest Walton, lived with his family at St Kevin's Park, off the Dartry Road. (Courtesy of Sean Duke)

Republican Army (IRA). Numerous stories are told about his heroism. Breen published an account of his guerrilla days, *My Fight for Irish Freedom*, in 1924. He represented his Tipperary constituency without a break until his retirement at the 1965 election. He died in 1969.

Another noteworthy resident was Irish-born Ernest Walton who in 1932 helped to split the atomic nucleus while working with Ernest Rutherford and John Cockroft in Cambridge University. The achievement was reported throughout the world. In 1951 Walton and Cockroft were awarded the Nobel Prize for Physics.

Walton returned to Ireland in 1934 to take up a position in Trinity College Dublin and because he wanted to marry his girlfriend Breda, who was working as a teacher in Waterford. They were married in Dublin and set about raising a family at their home in St Kevin's Park, in Dartry. Besides being a Professor of Natural and Experimental Philosophy in Trinity, he was involved with the Dublin Institute for Advanced Studies, the RDS, the Royal Irish Academy and many other eminent bodies.

He died in 1995, aged 92, and is remembered fondly by his colleagues and family as a quiet man who had no interest in being in the limelight. Visitors were often stunned to enter the staffroom at Trinity College Dublin and find Ernest Walton, the giant of physics who split the atom, sitting there, quietly humming a tune to himself.[108]

Between St Kevin's Park and Highfield Road is a striking enclave of tall red-brick houses dating from the early 1890s. This area is called Sunbury Gardens and has a small private park at the centre of the development. The houses are three-storey villas and were carefully designed so the two corner villas beside Dartry Road are the largest and have large conservatories. The villas farthest from the main road are not as impressive as these; they are far simpler and even lack the gables seen on the bigger houses.[109]

DROPPING DEAD AT THE WELL

Just down the hill from the Dartry Dye Works, with the bridge of arches in view, is the landmark Dropping Well pub by the riverside. It was built in 1847 on the site of a mortuary that was established to deal with dead bodies carried down the river to the pool underneath the nearby waterfall. It was later a well-known destination for 'bona fide' travellers who had to have gone more than 3 miles to be served a drink during the holy hour when Dublin pubs used to shut between 2.30 p.m. and 3.30 p.m. in the afternoon.

Dartry Road is also known as the scene of the still-controversial killing of IRA member Timothy Coughlin by police informer Seán Harling on the evening of 28 January 1928. The incident occurred opposite Woodpark Lodge, where Harling lived at the time.

12

ZION, BEWLEY'S AND BUSHY

Orwell Road is one of the main roads running through Rathgar. It connects to Zion and Bushy Park roads. Zion Road derives its name from the church on the corner rather than the Jewish community in Rathgar. It begins at Stratford College, from where one has a clear view of the Dublin Mountains along the road and behind the High School. Most of the older houses on Zion Road date from the 1860s, although Mayfield at no. 14 dates from 1849. The house was demolished, but the Mayfield address is still used for a modern terrace of luxury houses behind the original front garden wall. Zion Terrace (nos 9 to 23) was built in 1864. Valetta, at no. 7, is one of a terrace of three fine villas that date from 1867. A feature of Zion Road and part of Bushy

Bushy Park Road/Zion Road junction, Rathgar, with Zion Road church in background, 1900s. (Courtesy of Historic Pics Inc./Dulbin.ie Forums)

Park Road is the castellated granite front garden walls guarding the splendid houses. A six-foot wall protecting a house and picket-style railings in front of the houses near the entrance to the High School were originally erected to keep the cows on the farm from rambling out onto the road. The cows are gone but the grazing meadow remains as part of the playing pitches of the High School.

There used to be an interesting postbox on Zion Road on the corner with Victoria Road. It had the Victorian royal cypher on it. Pillarboxes were introduced into Rathgar from 1879 onwards. The initials 'V.R.' (which stands for 'Victoria Regina') were inscribed on this postbox and some others in Rathgar. The manufacturer, A. Handyside and Co. Ltd, Derby and London, was written around the base, indicating that the box was from between 1900 and 1904. Unfortunately, this historic box was removed and replaced with an uninteresting postbox, marked 'POST'. Some postboxes in Rathgar are inscribed 'E.R.', with VII incorporated, in honour of Queen Victoria's successor, King Edward VII. His reign lasted from 1901 to 1910. There are some examples of these on Rathgar Road (outside the former post office) and at the Kenilworth Road/Square junction. A Victorian wall box on Bushy Park Road, with the maker 'W.T. Allen, London', dates from 1882–85. It is opposite Rathgar House at nos 42–44. There are two other wall boxes: one on Dartry Road and the other on Orwell Road (outside the gate lodge to Marianella). The latter box is Victorian, the former has 'P 7 T' (Posts and Telegraphs) inscribed on it. Garville Avenue also has a 'P 7 T' postbox. Another box at the junction of Orwell Road and Gardens was also changed. This time the royal cypher was removed but 'A. Handyside, Derby & London' is still on its base. There is a low-sized Victorian postbox on Terenure Road East/Brighton Road corner. Orwell Park also boasts one. And just around the corner from the end of Frankfort Avenue, outside Fothergills, there is a postbox with GR inscribed. These old postboxes add to the character of Rathgar. The symbols of the postal service in the form of the crown and the royal insignia take their place alongside the signs of Irish independence: P 7 T and An Post.

There are three outstanding buildings amongst the fine, ornate and picturesque houses on Zion Road – Stratford College, Zion Road church (which in recently celebrated 150 years in Rathgar) and the High School.

Stratford College at 1 Zion Road was originally founded in 1954 by the Jewish community and is still under their auspices. The house dates from the early 1890s and was called Glengyle. The school today is a co-educational, fee-paying secondary school that derived its name from a house called 'Stratford' located around the corner on Terenure Road East, where the school was originally located. Glengyle was converted into a school and only the elegant mid-Victorian façade remains of the original structure. In the 1950s the Jewish community in the area was much larger than it is today and the student population of Stratford was entirely Jewish. Emigration took its toll and the board of management decided that the school should become multi-denominational, though it would retain its Jewish ethos.[110]

ERNEST BEWLEY AND THE HIGH SCHOOL

The letters 'DANVM' may be seen on one of the pillars of the main entrance gates to Rathgar High School ('DANVM' is the Latin spelling for Danum or Doncaster, where the former owner of the house was from). The impressive house was originally on 30 acres of farmland. It was built in 1906 by Ernest Bewley, proprietor of the famous Bewley's Oriental Cafés at Grafton and Westmoreland streets, who was the first occupant. The site was originally occupied by the Rathgar Sawmills, and located close to the River Dodder. The prosperity of the Bewley family enabled it to purchase the house and farm in Rathgar and use

The High School, Rathgar. The original school was in Harcourt Street before moving to Rathgar in 1951. One of its most famous pupils was the poet W.B. Yeats. (Courtesy of The High School)

the land for dairy cattle to supply the Dublin café's. Bewley (from a Quaker family involved in the importation of tea in the nineteenth century) originally opened Bewley's Oriental Café on Westmoreland Street. Such was the success of this exotic venture that other branches followed. Bewley's Café on Dublin's Grafton Street opened in 1927, and quickly became one of city's most distinctive and popular landmarks and meeting places. Its attractive interior is particularly noteworthy for the Harry Clarke stained-glass windows.

Danvm was divided into Danum Meadows and Danum Firs in the early 1940s. It remained in the Bewley family until the High School acquired it in the 1960s. It now covers twenty-two acres.[111]

Another reminder of the demolished house that was Danvm is the lodge at the entrance gates. The garden of this lodge contains a couple of cow troughs from the days when there was a dairy farm which supplied cream for Bewley's cafés. Just inside the entrance to the school itself, there is an impressive stained-glass-window memorial to those who fought in the world wars. Former pupils of the High School include poet and Nobel Prize winner W.B. Yeats, Irish government minister Alan Shatter and businessman Denis O'Brien. It has been said that O'Brien bought Doncaster FC as it reminded him of the name on the pillar of the High School.

VICTORIA ROAD

As the name suggests, Victoria Road, off Zion Road, is a road of red-brick houses dating from the latter part of that vanished era of the Empress of India. It is a model of tidy uniformity.

BUSHY PARK ROAD

Bushy Park Road links Terenure (and Bushy Park) to Zion Road and Rathgar. Less than half of this road is in Rathgar; the rest is in Terenure. The Rathgar section extends from Rathgar House at nos 42–44 on one side of the road to near the old Victorian wall postbox outside a lodge on the other side.

House-building started on Bushy Park Road in 1864, although Prospect House, at no. 48, dates from 1836 and Rathgar House dates from 1837. These two houses are shown on maps of the area for 1909 and are surrounded mainly by fields. Milverton, next door (no. 43), was built nearly a century later in 1927.

For many years, 12 Bushy Park Road, nearly opposite Zion Road church, was
the home of Robert Erskine Childers (1870–1922), who played a significant
role in Irish revolutionary history before and after the 1916 Rising. It was
his yacht, the *Asgard*, that smuggled 1,500 German Mauser rifles into Howth
Harbour in July 1914. An Englishman, he further embraced the Irish republican cause when, having been asked by Michael Collins and Éamon De Valera
to seek recognition for Ireland's claim for independence at the Paris Peace
Conference following the First World War, the claim was rejected. In June,
his family moved into the Bushy Park Road house. From here he travelled to
the Sinn Féin headquarters in Harourt Street. In 1921 he was appointed as
secretary for the Irish delegates during the Anglo-Irish Treaty negotiations in
London following the truce of the War of Independence. After the arrest of
Desmond Fitzgerald, Erskine Childers was appointed Minister of Propaganda in
February 1921. He worked from May Langan's house on nearby Victoria Road,
with his staff in his own house on Bushy Park Road. He subsequently joined
the anti-Treaty side. He died during the Civil War that followed the signing
of the Anglo-Irish Treaty; he was shot in 1922 by Irish Free State forces in
Beggars Bush Barracks in Dublin. His son, also named Erskine Childers, lived
for many years on Highfield Road and later became President of Ireland.[112]

ERSKINE CHILDERS

A President for all the nation.

"The Presidency is the highest office in the land. I firmly believe that it should give a lead to the nation at the highest level – in matters like the quality of life, the development of our unique culture and the enhance- ment of our image abroad. To stimulate thinking about ourselves and how we wish to live in the future, to encourage the setting up of long range goals to be aimed at, to listen to the dreams of the young with the wisdom of experience – these are among the functions of a President. To perform them properly requires consider- able experience of national and international affairs, a background of culture and a high degree of personal integrity. I know you will find these qualities in Erskine Childers. When you vote on Wednesday, consider them and his long record of personal service to the Nation.'

Jack Lynch.

Published by Anthony Dudley, Solr., 51 Fitzwilliam Sq., Dublin 2. Agent for the candidate.

Election literature of Fianna Fáil for presidential candidate Erskine Childers, who subsequently became the fourth President of Ireland. He lived on Highfield Road for many years. (Courtesy of FF)

Photograph of Erskine Hamilton Childers on the occasion of his inauguration as President of Ireland, 25 June 1973, at Dublin Castle. Also pictured are Mrs Rita Childers and former president, Eamon de Valera. (Courtesy of NAI, Department of the Taoiseach, 2004/21/518)

Robert Erskine Childers (1870-1922) toward the end of his life. He wrote many books including the best-selling *The Riddle of the Sands* (1903). Robert Erskine Childers made an immense contribution to the foundation of the Irish State. His family continued to play a role in Irish public life following his death with his son Erskine Hamilton Childers becoming President of Ireland and his grand-daughter Nessa an MEP. (Courtesy of fotofinish)

Just beyond the boundary where Rathgar meets Terenure is Riversdale House, a country-style retreat on the banks of the River Dodder and the home for many years of the renowned editor of *The Irish Times* (1963–86), Douglas Gageby (1918–2004). When one proceeds through the original wrought-iron gates of the driveway, one sees three properties. Gageby built another Riversdale House beside the original one in 1965, as well as a smaller property called The Barn. The properties have a tucked-away, rural feel to them in their quiet leafy enclave, with an old and enormous chestnut tree in the large front garden, and yet they are quite close to Rathgar village.

Many of the residents of Rathgar would have been readers of *The Irish Times*, which for many years was regarded as an organ of Unionism in Ireland. Under Gageby, it developed a more nationalist hue and tone. He was regarded as the pre-eminent Irish newspaper editor of his generation. His daughter is Susan Denham, Chief Justice of the Supreme Court of Ireland.[113]

Bushy Park Road was also the home of Dr George Mullett (1937–2000), one of Ireland's preeminent psychiatrists. Dr Mullett, consultant psychiatrist in St James' and St Patrick's Hospitals, and clinical teacher in the Department of Psychiatry, Trinity College, is remembered annually by the George Mullett Prize for clinical excellence awarded to students of psychiatry in TCD.

THE RATHGAR CIRCLE

Arnold Bax (1883–1953), the English composer and poet, moved to Ireland in 1911 with his new wife and rented a villa on Bushy Park Road for a short time. In his autobiography, he described the views from the back windows of the incongruously named Yeovil:

> there was ... a clear vista of park-like wooded country and beyond that of the complete ring of the untamed Dublin Mountains. On any clear day one's eye could wander along that amphitheatre of beloved slopes, over Niall Glundubh's cairn on Tibradden, past haunted Kilmashogue, down into the sylvan hollows of Glendhu, up again along a red-brown fringe of leafless trees to the sinister ruins of Kilakee brooding over Dublin's south-western suburbs – the Hellfire Club, monumental to the arrogance and violence of the eighteenth-century Irish gentry – until finally one's gaze rested upon Seefin, a pearl-grey phantasm of a mountain, its summit gleaming maybe with the snowdrifts of last week's blizzard. And deep in those folded

hills, thirty miles away, was hidden Glendalough of the Seven Churches, an enchanted place of holy gloom.[114]

Having settled in Rathgar, Bax's brother Clifford introduced Arnold and his wife to the intellectual circle which met at the Rathgar Avenue house of the poet, painter and mystic, George Russell (Æ). Bax had already had some of his poems and short stories published in Dublin. To others in the circle he was simply known as Dermot O'Byrne. As Dermot O'Byrne, he was specifically noted for *Seafoam and Firelight*, published in London in 1909, and numerous short stories and poems published in different media in Dublin. It was at Russell's house that Bax met one of the future leaders of the 1916 Rising, Pádraig Pearse. According to Bax, they got on very well and, although they met only once, the execution of Pearse following the Rising prompted Bax to compose several laments, the most noted being *In Memoriam Patrick Pearse* (1916), which contains the dedication '*I gCuimhne ar Phádraig Mac Piarais*' (In Memory of Padraig Pearse).

The war led to the dissolution of the Rathgar Circle as many members fled Ireland and Europe. Bax and his family returned to London.[115]

13

GROSVENOR, KENILWORTH AND THE GOTHIC

GROSVENOR ROAD – CARSON AND BECKETT

For many years until the mid-1850s Grimwood's Nurseries was located close to the junction of Rathgar Road, Grosvenor Road and Rathmines Road. The nurseries occupied approximately 15 acres of land. This was an excellent location for Grimwood's, as the underground River Swan ran close by and its water was essential for the growing of plants and vegetables to supply some of Dublin's needs. A painting by Cecilia Nairn from 1817 shows a pathway leading to the nurseries with a river and the Dublin Mountains in the background. There was a small nursery at Highfield Road as recently as 2005. Even before the 1850s, however, Dublin's developers had started to plan for the building of Grosvenor and Kenilworth roads on the Grimwood's lands.

Grosvenor Road has a variety of Victorian architecture, with houses designed and built by Edward Henry Carson (father of the Ulster Unionist leader Edward Carson who was born at the family's home on Harcourt Street), George Palmer Beater, and James and William Beckett (William was the grandfather of Samuel Beckett). Some of the Grosvenor Road houses date from as early as 1840, with Rosetta, at no. 26, built in that year, Grosvenor House (no. 2) in 1848 (although there is another, newer Grosvenor House across the road) and Rathmore (no. 19) in 1852. The majority, however, date from the 1860s. The picturesque grey Baptist church overlooking the roundabout (known as the Diamond) at the junction of Grosvenor Road and Grosvenor Place was built in 1859.

Beside the church, at no. 17, is Gosford (home of William Acheson, related to the earls of Gosford, a goldsmith, watchmaker and jeweller with premises on Grafton Street). It was designed by Edward Carson and has Gothic, Swiss and Byzantine influences. Number 18, home to St Michael's House, is a fine, detached, ornate red-brick building. St Michael's is part of an organisation that has been catering for the needs of children with Down's syndrome since 1955, having been founded by Patricia Farrell, a farmer from County Westmeath. Number 20 is of a different yet elegant style; it was designed by George William Beater, who was influenced by the Gothic Revival style.[116]

Across from the church, the detached St Brendan's (no. 15) dates from 1860. It overlooks the roundabout and is built on a substantial plot of land. It attracted much attention and offers of up to €15 million during the Celtic Tiger era. Woburn House was built in 1864, as was Tavistock (no. 39). Thornville (no. 16) dates from 1862. Westminster (no. 10) dates from 1860, as does Wakefield (no. 7). Alma House (no. 18) dates from 1860. Two large three-storey semi-detached houses, nos 26 and 27, dating from around 1859, with flights of steps leading up to the front doors, occupy the corner facing toward Rathgar Road. No. 27 was the home for many years of the McBirney sisters, from the family that owned the famous department store, McBirney's, located on Dublin's Aston Quay. This fine three-storey house with large hall and drawing and sitting rooms and commanding a view along Grosvenor Road to Rathgar Road, retains a well-maintained garden of approximately one-third of an acre. The garden of the adjoining house, no. 26, also being a corner property, was used in the mid-twentieth century to build a short terrace of houses that is Grosvenor Villas and which leads to the eclectic enclave that is Bushes Lane and also to the grounds of the Ashbrook Tennis Club.

Particularly attractive are the line of ten detached villas, nos 66 to 75, which stretch from the Rathmines end of Grosvenor Road up to the Diamond. Most of these were built in the mid-1860s, although Laurel Bank, at no. 70, dates from 1906 and Hughenden (no. 67) dates from 1896. Number 73 was once home to Professor Andrew Francis ('Anatomy Dick') Dixon. Revd Charles William Benson (1836–1919), headmaster of the famous Rathmines School, lived at 65 Grosvenor Road from 1865 to 1880. Farther along the road, nos 53–56 were described by the architectural historian Jeremy Williams as 'the most ambitious Gothic Revival speculative terrace built in the Dublin suburbs; designed in the rather spikey Gothic idiom employed by both A.G. Jones and E.H. Carson'. These houses have four levels and prominent bow windows. Entrances are accessed by flights of steps.[117]

Besides the detached villas, there are many two- and three-storey over-garden-level residences with elegant iron railings and sweeping granite stairs leading to the front doors.

An unusual feature of houses nos 35–39 is the small sculpted heads above each of the front-door fanlights. Each of these mostly male heads has a different expression and one wears a crown. The only female head has a halo-like structure on its head. The story is told that the reason for only one female head is that when the builder was refurbishing the property in 1997 he was unable to find a replacement head for the missing male one and had to opt for the present head instead.

The old Fenian John O'Leary lived at several different addresses in Rathgar, including 30 Grosvenor Road for a time.

KENILWORTH ROAD AND SQUARE – PERIOD DETAILS AND PIGEONS

The builder Michael Murphy was prominent in developing this part of Rathgar. The square itself was supposed to be a communal pleasure garden similar to the one at Harold's Cross and Palmerston parks, but it never materialised. Kenilworth Road and Square houses date from 1860, although Dudley Lodge, at 44 Kenilworth Square, had been built in 1846. Kenilworth Villa at the junction of Grosvenor Place and Kenilworth Road was built in 1860, as was Kenilworth House at 3 Kenilworth Square. This outstanding double-fronted house overlooks the square. Warwick House, at 31 Kenilworth Square, dates from 1862, as does Leicester House at no. 75. The four houses of Waverly Terrace (including one called Waverly Ville) at the junction with Harold's Cross Road and Kenilworth Road were built in 1879. Glenmalure at 56 Kenilworth Square was not built until 1927. The terrace of houses at 1–8 Kenilworth Road has its own private road parallel to the main road.[118]

When 20 Kenilworth Road was put up for sale in 2015, prospective buyers saw that most of the period details were in excellent condition (the house had been unoccupied for many years and, unlike some other houses, had never been converted into flats). The intricate coving in the main rooms and the hallway is typical of this type of house in Rathgar and has three strata, which feature egg and dart, ivy and berry details. Prior to putting the property on the market, however, the vendors had to deal with 300 pigeons nesting in the house and the 2-foot deep deposit of guano on the attic floor![119]

LIONS AND GRACIOUS LIVING

Kenilworth Square was built in stages by different builders. The developer of one terrace in the 1860s built no. 18 for himself so it is grander in scale and detailing than its neighbours. At one time it would have had stables at the rear, hence the double entrance gates at the side of the house, but the stables were sold long ago for a mews. Elegant rooms of grand proportions and period features, including high ceilings, cornices, cherubs and much more, are prominent in this house and many of the houses on the square.

A lion stands guard outside no. 6 Kenilworth Square. This is not the only lion; another stands guard outside no. 31 and no. 13 has two lions standing at the foot of the steps leading up to the entrance. Outside this latter dwelling, in the front garden, there is an ornate lamp standard with five lamps. The words 'Annefield Terrace' are emblazoned over this red-brick terrace of six houses, which have bay windows and stucco door entrances in the classical style. These houses have a fine view of the green playing fields of Kenilworth Square itself.

The square is divided into four sections – north, south, east and west – with corresponding addresses. Parts of the neighbouring roads also share some of the square's addresses, e.g., Kenilworth Square South extends nearly halfway down Leicester Avenue, with the older three-storey red-bricks seemingly looking down on the two-storeys opposite. There is another unusual feature: two adjacent houses in the area share the same number. Number 1 Kenilworth Square is beside 1 Kenilworth Road. Residents of the square were keyholders to the park for many years, up until about fifteen years ago when the owners of the park, St Mary's College, Rathmines (who use the grounds as rugby playing pitches for their students), withdrew the privilege. Kenilworth Lane consists of converted mews dwellings built on the back gardens of houses along Kenilworth Road and Square.

There are some impressive houses overlooking the square. Number 3 has been described as an 'elegant symmetrical Greek Revival'.[120] Number 75 is a spectacular design. Numbers 83 and 84, dating from around 1859, stand out because of the architectural gems on display. These two houses were originally built to look like one. However, a latter-day architect noted that this is 'a curious example of a pair of semi-detached houses treated to look like an asymmetrical Gothic revival villa. The execution did not match up to the concept.'[121]

Of course this view is highly debatable and is contrary to a widespread appreciation of these unique and impressive houses. The present owners have done much to preserve the integrity of the original design, details and structure, built over 150 years ago, even going so far as to incorporate a 'V' into the glass shape of a top-floor window to complement other similar design structures in one of the houses.

FROM BOOKS TO BOWLING

Kenilworth Square was the home for many years of the Kenilworth Bowling Club. The club originated in a meeting of influential upper-class gentlemen in 1892 at the house of Charles Eason (of Eason bookshops) who owned nos 29/30. The first members appear to have been prosperous businessmen and included several of English and Scottish origin. Membership was limited to those from those of high social standing, including the Lord Lieutenant and Chief Secretary for Ireland. The Annual Ball, a most elaborate event, was held in Rathmines Town Hall. The club used the location until the 1920s when it was decided to move to nearby Grosvenor Square. One of the reasons being that the club's grounds were used for football and other sports during the winter and this damaged the quality of the playing greens. St Mary's College, Rathmines then used the park as the college sports grounds and in 1947 a decision was made to purchase it. The college continues to use the grounds to this day.[122]

TO READ OR NOT TO READ – THAT WAS THE QUESTION

Eason's (which is still going strong and has branches throughout Ireland) was originally founded in 1819 as Johnston & Co. Since then, it has witnessed some of the most exciting events in Irish history and has grown to become the main supplier of books, newspapers and magazines in Ireland. It was in 1886, during the heady days of Parnell and the Land League, that Charles Eason and his son acquired the business from W.H. Smith.

Over the course of the nineteenth century, the company was directly involved in the revolution in the public's reading habits. Its railway bookstalls became popular, a popularity which depended on a growing literacy rate. More people could read, so written information became more important to the country as a whole. By 1860, the *Freeman's Journal* was selling more than a thousand copies a day through Eason's distribution network and *The Irish Times* nearly double that. Thirty years later, these figures had quadrupled. However, with the infiltration of English culture through English newspapers

This amazing scene from 26 June 1932 is the closing ceremony of the Eucharistic Congress that was held in Dublin in June 1932. Earlier in the day, there had been a Solemn Pontifical High Mass at 1 p.m. in Phoenix Park, with a special choir of 500 men and boys. A procession, estimated at one million people and described as 'miles of praying people', then made its way to O'Connell Bridge. The Service of Benediction and Hymns on O'Connell Bridge took place around 5.30 p.m., and the Papal Legate Cardinal Lorenzo Lauri gave his final address of the Eucharistic Congress from this location. The main individual responsible for organising the Congress was Frank O'Reilly who lived at Kenilworth Square. (Courtesy GCI/fotofinish)

Frank O'Reilly, secretary of the CTSI, who organised the 1932 Eucharistic Congress in Dublin. Here he has just been awarded an Honorary Doctorate by the National University of Ireland after the Congress. (Courtesy of Dublin Diocesan Archives) and the 'penny dreadfuls' (cheap books), alarm bells sounded and advocates of a more Irish Ireland during the Celtic Revival went on the offensive, promoting alternatives with an Irish, Catholic viewpoint. This ultimately led to the censorship of publications campaign of the 1920s.[123]

Francis T. O'Reilly was another resident of Kenilworth. He lived on the corner of the square at 1 Kenilworth Road and was one of the most important individuals in twentieth-century Irish history, yet he remains relatively unknown. He was the organising genius behind both the 1929 Catholic emancipation centenary celebrations and the Eucharistic Congress of 1932. Most importantly, he, as head of the Catholic Truth Society of Ireland (CTSI, now Veritas) spearheaded the campaign of the 1920s for stringent censorship of literature, which culminated in the Censorship of Publications Act, 1929. Over the course of this campaign, O'Reilly had to reprimand Eason's for not supporting strengthening legislation against objectionable literature. Following the Eucharistic Congress, he returned to relative obscurity with the CTSI. He died in 1957.[124]

DEV AND THE TREATY

One of the houses on the west side of Kenilworth Square provided the setting for the film of Maeve Binchy's novel *Tara Road*. The Rathgar Hotel, at 33–34 Kenilworth Square, became the Mungret Guest House in 1960 before it was converted back to a hotel. It subsequently reverted to private use.

In 1921, during the War of Independence, Éamon de Valera's office was moved to 53 Kenilworth Square when his house in Blackrock was raided. It was in this house that Arthur Griffith presented Lloyd George's proposals for the Anglo-Irish Treaty to de Valera four days before the Treaty was signed in London.

Other well-known residents of this house included the Le Brocquy family; Sybil and Albert moved there from 4 Zion Road in 1931. The family owned the Greenmount Oil Company in Harold's Cross. Sybil wrote poems and plays and was president of the Irish Women Writers' Society and was also involved in the Yeats Association, as well as being the organiser of the Synge centennial celebrations. Her son Louis Le Brocquy is acclaimed as one of the foremost Irish artists of the twentieth century. One of his most famous and popular paintings, *A Family* (1951), is now in the National Gallery of Ireland.

Ernest Blythe (1889–1975), TD and senator, was successively Minister for Finance, Minister for Post & Telegraphs, and Minister for Trade & Commerce.

He lived at 50 Kenilworth Square from 1940 until his death in 1975. Blythe was born in County Antrim, where he was a government clerk and reporter for the *North Down Herald*. He was an unusual figure in Ireland's fight for independence, being a Protestant Unionist. A Gaelic Leaguer, Blythe advocated violence to achieve political means and was an Irish Volunteer organiser. In 1918 he became a Sinn Féin TD for North Monaghan before becoming Minister for Finance in 1922 and then Vice President of the Executive Council (deputy head of government). From 1941 to 1967 he was managing director of the Abbey Theatre.

CHAMPIONS OF BALLADEERS AND INDEPENDENT CINEMA

Another famous resident was Peggy Jordan (1918-2000) who did much to help launch ballad groups such as The Dubliners and the Clancy Brothers. The parties and ballad sessions in her home at Kenilworth Square were renowned.[125]

A well-known figure who lived on the square was Albert (Alby) Kelly (1924–2005), a champion of independent cinema during the 1970s and 1980s.

The former Classic cinema on Harold's Cross Road, near the home of owner and manager, Albert Kelly, who lived at Kenilworth Square. (Courtesy of Classic)

He successfully lobbied the government to reduce the VAT charged on cinema tickets and also to have city and suburban cinemas treated equally with regard to new film releases. Hitherto, suburban cinemas had to wait three months before they were allowed to show the major film releases. He was the owner of the famous Classic (formerly 'The Kenilworth') cinema on the Harold's Cross Road, near his home. One of the most popular films shown here was *The Rocky Horror Picture Show*, which ran for over twenty-one years. The Friday showings of this cult film involved many of the audience singing and throwing rice in the air. He continued working until he was nearly eighty, and only retired, reluctantly, on doctor's orders.'[126]

ONE OF IRELAND'S TOP HOTELIERS

Wilhelm (always known as 'Willy') Ludwig Oppermann (1928–2001) lived at Kenilworth Square and Orwell Park for many years. He was regarded as one of Ireland's foremost hoteliers.

Well-known Dublin hotelier, Wilhelm (Willy) Oppermann (1928-2001), was born at Kenilworth Square and subsequently lived at Orwell Park.

Willy was the second youngest of his family. He was born when the family lived at Kenilworth Square. He went to school in Synge Street. As a young man Willy had a keen interest acting and was a member of the Rathmines and Rathgar Musical Society. On one occasion he took part in *The Mikado* in the Rathmines Town Hall.

After leaving school Willy went into the catering business and was Manager in a number of Dublin hotels, including the International Hotel in Bray, the Moira Hotel off Dame Street, Jury's Hotel when it was located on Dame Street, the Dolphin Hotel and the Burlington Hotel. During his career, Willy travelled abroad on many occasions as part of Bord Fáilte delegations, promoting Ireland as a place to visit. In 1969 Willy, together with his brother Johnny, purchased a property in Kilternan, where they built the Oppermann Hotel and Country Club. The family is still in the hotel business.[127]

14

JAMES JOYCE'S OLD TRIANGLE

FROM CROMWELL TO BRIGHTON

That long tree-lined road filled with Victorian red-brick houses that extends from Rathgar Road to Brighton Square is called Brighton Road. House styles on the road vary. The larger and older three-storey houses with flights of steps leading up to the entrances are on one side. Facing them are the mainly two-storey, bay-windowed houses, called the 'new houses' by some of the older residents. The older houses, nos 47–52, have the name 'Trevelyn' emblazoned over the terrace.

Mark Bentley was the property developer of the Brighton Road and Square area. That he knew little of Ireland is evidenced by the fact that he named one of the new roads as 'Cromwell Road'. It is listed in the 1863 and 1864 *Thom's Directories* with three houses, all vacant. Eventually someone must have told him that, however, highly regarded he might be in England, the name Oliver Cromwell was most unpopular in Ireland. He therefore changed the name to Brighton Road, a natural companion for the square and avenue already built. Thereafter, he had no problem and by 1868 there were fifteen houses occupied in Brighton Road, with just three vacant.[128]

Some of the houses on Brighton Road are particularly significant. Number 11 Brighton Road is celebrated in James Joyce's *Ulysses* as it is the home of Mat Dillon. Felix Hackett lived at 46 Brighton Road from 1911–22. He was Professor of Physics and Electrical Engineering at UCD from 1926–52 and later President of the RDS. The family moved from Brighton Road to 20 Zion Road in 1922.

A young James Joyce in 1884 while living at Brighton Square, Rathgar. (Courtesy of GCI)

Probably the same developer who had tried to convince people to buy houses on Cromwell Road also hoped to use the name for Upper Garville Avenue. He soon changed this to Kensington Road, but by 1865 he found it convenient to change it again to Upper Garville Avenue, a name which, incidentally, was applied also to the south side of Brighton Square on some Ordnance Survey maps of the time. Kensington Lodge, one of the houses on the road, acts as a reminder of the street's former name.

THE DISCREET CHARM OF BRIGHTON SQUARE

Brighton Road opens on to Brighton Square, which is one of the last of Dublin's Victorian squares still under private ownership (as is Kenilworth Square), most of the others having been turned over to the local authorities long ago. As one of the privileges of living in the area, the residents of the square have their own keys to the square's park and may enjoy the tennis courts, vegetable garden, play area and markets.

The park has a picket fence and is full of old chestnut trees. It also contains a wooden tennis pavilion, a large cottage-style structure with 'Wm. Spence Memorial 1908' over the entrance. William Spence lived at 68/69 Brighton Square and was a prominent engineer and iron founder in Dublin. His firm, based in Cork Street in the Liberties, flourished. It manufactured machinery for breweries, distilleries, corn and flour mills, as well as steam engines and boilers and constructional ironwork. He died in 1907 and there was an account of his funeral in *The Irish Times*.[129]

Number 41 Brighton Square, the house where James Joyce was born, overlooks the square. He was born 2 February 1882. His mother, May Murray, was born in 1859 in Terenure, in what is now Vaughan's pub.

James Joyce played in the park across the road as a child. In fact, in suitably Joycean fashion, Brighton Square is not a square at all, but a triangle. However, 'triangle' does not sound quite as elegant as 'square'. Around the triangular park stands a guard of solid red-brick houses, some with bay windows, some without, some three storeys high, some two. Numbers 17 and 18 have eye-catching doorways with two carved stucco heads on their frames. These grim faces with

James Joyce's birthplace at 41 Brighton Square, Rathgar. Notice the commemorative plaque between the upper two windows. The plaque was unveiled on 6 June 1964. (Courtesy of GCI)

Birth and baptismal certificate of James Joyce, with an address of 41 Brighton Square, Terenure. In fact, Brighton Square is in Rathgar, but the church where he was baptised is in Terenure. (Courtesy of BMD Office)

huge ears create a startling effect. The square is encircled by original ornate street lamps with shamrocks over the lights. These were made at the famous Hammond Lane Foundry in Dublin in the early twentieth century.

Joyce considered his birthday to be an auspicious day and he liked to tie events in his life to his own birthday or the birthdays of friends and family. On the occasion of his forty-ninth birthday in 1931, Joyce received a birthday letter from his father in which John Joyce reminded him of 'the old days in Brighton Square, when you were Babie Tuckoo, and I used to take you out in the Square and tell you about the moo-cow that used to come down from the mountain and take little boys across'.[130]

According the Joycean scholar Peter Costello, his father bringing him to the park made a lasting impression on the baby Joyce. That and the sweet shop owned by Betty Byrne in a nearby lane. After his birth, the Joyces remained at Brighton Square for a further two years, before moving to nearby Rathmines. The Joyce family was friends with the Dillons and Murrays on nearby

Brighton Road. Matthew Dillon, the inspiration for 'Mat Dillon' of *Ulysses*, lived in a red-brick Victorian house at 11 Brighton Road with his happy family, 'a bevy of girls', as Joyce describes them. In the book, Joyce's character, Leopold Bloom, recalls the Dillons' large, lilac-filled garden and the gaiety and laughter of the girls playing and rambling about on the summer lawns.[131]

While they lived in Brighton Square, the Joyces were frequent attendees at the nearby Church of the Three Patrons on Rathgar Road, which was also recalled in *Ulysses*. Not only did they attend Mass and the various Catholic ceremonies and devotions; they were also part of the church choir.[132]

Costello has written much on Joyce's early years, in particular those years spent in Brighton Square. In a talk given by Costello on Joyce on Bloomsday, 16 June 2004, he stated that the Rathgar world Joyce knew was one of croquet parties, tennis-club dances, afternoon tea and respectability. The girls wore tea

Elsie Thompson Harrison of Brighton Square, Dublin, in her nursing uniform, most likely taken during the First World War. Her family are listed on the 1911 census as owning a hardware business and as being part of the Plymouth Brethern – an evangelical movement established in Dublin in the 1820s. Her brother had the unusual name of Gordon Trizzant Harrison. (Courtesy of Orla Fitzpatrick/Jacolette/Wordpress)

A typical Rathgar family when James Joyce was living at Brighton Square. (Courtesy of Orla FitzpatrickJacolette/Wordpress)

dresses and bonnets and the young men played rugby and cricket. The ladies were 'at home' during certain hours to receive callers and the men were starched and upright and worried about their place in 'society'. Costello noted that the Dublin bourgeoisie of that time was fashioned after the English late-Victorian and Edwardian model. Although it was not as formal as London, its intercourse was still based on a strict code of one's 'connections' and perceived standing.

Joyce, then, was as much a product of this Anglified class as he was of his Irish, Celtic side. He was profoundly influenced by his father's determination to be a 'gentleman'.[133]

Today, James Joyce's Bloomsday is celebrated in his birthplace, Rathgar, with readings, music on the road, food and wine, and various other events and activities in Rathgar village each year on 16 June.

Brighton Avenue, linking the square to Rathgar Avenue, contains an eclectic variety of styles of residences, including attractive one-storey cottage-type houses. It also dates from 1864, with building continuing until the 1890s. Rosslyn Cottage, at no. 22, dates from 1886.

15

SPORT
AND MUSIC

Rathgar has many sporting venues. Cricket, tennis and bowling were very popular in Rathgar towards the end of the nineteenth century. Bowling must be the oldest activity practised in the area, having started with the Kenilworth Bowling Club. Bowling is still played at the Rathgar Tennis and Bowling Club in Herzog Park on Orwell Road. This club has over 1,000 members and it was where Irish rugby star Jonathan Sexton met his future bride, Laura. They both played tennis at the club.

Tennis has a long connection with Rathgar, starting with the Mount Temple Tennis Club in the late nineteenth century. It closed in 1961 and members, including the renowned Irish tennis player Gerry Fitzpatrick, transferred to the Elm Park Tennis Club. Other tennis clubs open today include the Brookfield (dating from 1906) near Highfield and Dartry roads and the Ashbrook, off Grosvenor Road, which has been in existence since 1922.

One of Dublin's best-kept secrets, the Ashbrook originally started in Kimmage. It moved to Rathgar in 1927. Moving was not easy; the members carried the pavilion by horse, cart and bicycle to the new grounds. A theatrical group was also established and the young Milo O'Shea and Maureen Potter received some of their first laughs at the pavilion. Dances were run on Saturday nights from the 1950s until the 1970s. In 1967 Ashbrook hosted the Irish Open Championship, the first and only Irish club to host the championship outside the Fitzwillam LTC.[134]

Hockey is played at the High School sports grounds on Orwell Road and rugby and cricket are played at the High School and St Mary's grounds on Kenilworth Square.

THE R&R

Dublin has always been a musical city. It had many musical societies in the early decades of the twentieth century. It also had music halls, such as the Empire Palace and the Tivoli, the Antient Concert Rooms and the Theatre Royal, which had seating for nearly 2,500 people. The present-day Olympia Theatre was originally Dan Lowrey's Music Hall. The Gaiety Theatre opened in 1872 and became famous for its annual pantomime.

One of the most famous musical societies is the Rathgar and Rathmines Musical Society, which is still going strong. Affectionately known as 'the R&R', this society has the unique distinction of being the only musical society in continuous existence, producing two, maybe three, shows a year in the principal theatres of Dublin and the National Concert Hall without interruption since 1913. With over 100 years under its belt, the R&R has produced over 250 shows, with approximately 2,600 performances. It all started in 1913 at a meeting held at 48 Summerville Park in Rathmines. C.P. Fitzgerald, who

Rathmines and Rathgar Musical Society.

FIRST SEASON   -   1913 - 1914.

CONCERT

TOWN HALL, RATHMINES.

22nd April, 1914.

Book of Words.

One of early programmes for the R&R Musical Society. (Courtesy of R&R)

was the young organist in Rathgar's Church of the Three Patrons at that time, wanted to establish a musical society. He persuaded a group of friends to form a musical society, and, as they all lived in Rathgar or Rathmines, the society was christened accordingly. Fitzgerald was the conductor, Edwin Lloyd, a solicitor from Kenilworth Square, was chairman, W.G. Mulvin of York Road was honorary secretary and J.C. O'Brien of Belgrave Square was the producer. The businessman William Martin Murphy of Dartry Hall became president. By the end of 1913, the society was sufficiently organised to book the Gaiety Theatre for a production of Gilbert & Sullivan's *The Mikado* in December.[135]

The following year, also in December, the society performed for the first time in the Gaiety Theatre with another Gilbert & Sullivan operetta, *Yeomen of the Guard*. In 1915 Planquette's *Les Cloches de Corneville* was performed. This broadening of the society's range of productions afforded its members

Well-known RTÉ broadcaster Gay Byrne chatting with some of the cast of the R&R Musical Society in Dublin's Mansion House during the centenary celebrations in 2013. (Courtesy of R&R)

many different opportunities to use their individual and combined range of musical talents and dramatic skills.

The society has, since its establishment all those years ago, become a major contributor to the musical-theatre life of Dublin city. It also has a long and happy association with the Feis Ceoil. In 1946, the R&R presented a cup to be awarded for the best performance of a song from any light opera. Later, the Ford Taylor prize was established for the best performance of a Gilbert & Sullivan work.

Famous members who went on to become professionals include Frank Fay and Ria Mooney (Abbey Theatre), David Kelly, Jack MacGowran, T.P. McKenna and Terry Wogan.[136]

BURIED BUT VERY MUCH ALIVE!

Some interesting facts about the R&R include the fact that Count Casimir Markieviez, husband of Constance Gore-Booth (Countess Markievicz), took part in the 1914 production of *Yeomen of the Guard* at the Gaiety Theatre. He rang the bell in the funeral scene finale of Act 1. Brian Hayes TD also appeared in a play: the 1998 production of *Fiddler on the Roof*.

Legends of the Gaiety Theatre: Jimmy O'Dea with Maurieen Potter in 1964. (Courtesy of RTÉ/fotofinish)

On 22 April 1914 the R&R gave a concert in Rathmines Town Hall. One of the performers was Owen Lloyd, a noted harpist (whose son Edwin was the first chairman of the R&R). Owen taught the harp at Pádraig Pearse's school, St Enda's.

In 1989, Dublin's Lord Mayor Seán Haughey buried a time capsule in North Earl Street. The capsule contains the R&R 75th Anniversary Record and other material relevant to the society's activities, together with a covering memorandum setting out the history of the society and its contribution to the cultural life of the city.

The R&R made its way into fiction when it was mentioned in *At Swim Two Birds* by Flann O'Brien in 1939.[137]

16

RATHGAR VILLAGE – SHOPS AND BUSINESSES

Rathgar village developed because it was at the junction of farm laneways near one of the main entrances to Rathgar Castle. Weston St John Joyce wrote in 1912 that 'on Orwell Road, about 80 yards from the tram track, are the massive pillars of a gateway' (of the original castle). An inn and some thatched cottages had earlier been built at the crossroads. The area was known for many years as The Thatch.[138]

Rathgar remains one of Dublin's distinctive old villages. To this day, it hosts a beautiful array of quaint shops and restaurants and has an attractive, village-like atmosphere.

Some of the Rathgar villlage shops. (Courtesy of GCI)

Rathgar village in the early twentieth century. (Courtesy of Rathgar Presbyterian church)

The Gourmet Shop is a third-generation delicatessen, which happily sits along-side a bicycle shop, two craft butchers (Donovan's and Byrne's, long-established family businesses), designer boutiques, a travel agency, the Rathgar Bookshop, an antique shop, The Vintry and O'Brien's wine shops, a photographer's, a chemist's, a flower shop, a supermarket and a collection of favourite restaurants, including The Bijou, Mizzonni's and Howard's Way. The Auto Restorers business around the corner at the top of Rathgar Avenue, with its old clock (always showing three o'clock) over the entrance, is also an old family business. And of course the village would not be complete without a Butler's Pantry. Until recently, Deveney's shop and the Monument Creamery were also in the village.

It is also home to solicitors, accountants, financial advisors and several other businesses, including the landmark building containing Allied Irish Bank and, across the road, Comans pub, which dates from 1847. Moreover, the location of the impressive church at the junction of Rathgar and Highfield roads makes it a particularly beautiful focal point in the village.

VILLAGE LIFE IN ELEGANT TIMES

The well-known writer, barrister and raconteur Ulick O'Connor was born and raised in Rathgar. He remembers the area as 'middle-class, stand-offish but not

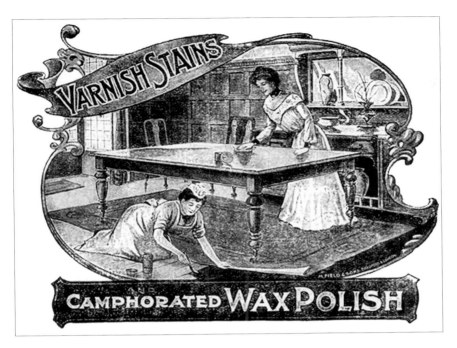

This turn-of-the-century advertisement for polish shows a housewife and her housemaid working in harmony; the lady cleans the table while the housemaid engages in the much more strenuous task of staining the floorboards. At this time most middle-class housewives would have had a least one servant to help with the heavy work of washing and cleaning. Depending on the degree of wealth, a household could have up to four servants. (Courtesy of GCI)

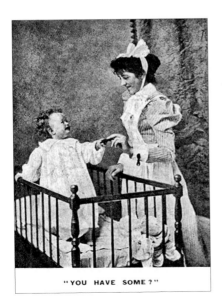

"YOU HAVE SOME?"

The Nursemaid. Advertisement from *The Dublin Horse Show Annual*, 1901. This advertisement shows a wealthy child and his nursemaid, smiling, healthy and clean, in sharp contrast to many Dublin children of the time. In wealthy families discipline was strict and in many cases children had little contact with their parents. Children of wealthy families were cared for by servants; initially by nursery maids and afterwards by nannies. The nurses and nannies, who could begin their working life as young as 13 and who played such an important role in these households, could be summarily dismissed and disappear from a child's life. (Courtesy of GCI)

Drawing Room in Model House.

This page from Thom's Directory shows the ideal of middle-class living in the Dublin of 1913. While the furniture has lost the highly decorated legs of the Victorian era, the window, with inset seat, is still heavily draped. The image is from an advertisement for James Hill and Sons, 10-12 Bacherlor's Walk, who in 1913 were offering to furnish a full house, including the servant's bedroom, for the sum of £125. (Courtesy of GCI)

snobbish'. He happily recalls the Gilbert & Sullivan musical evenings in people's front rooms and going to the opera. They were 'elegant' times, he recalls. Patrick Byrne, of Byrne's Family Butchers, recalls 'Lady Hogan', who used to go around the area on her High Nelly bicycle, cleaning the steps and brasses of the fine houses. A gathering of nannies at the village junction was a frequent sight. Most houses would have had nannies to look after the growing children. The nannies would all meet near the Presbyterian church and parade down Highfield Road to Palmerston Park with their prams and children.

In times gone by, grocers and provision dealers were the main shops in the village and on the corner of Frankfort Avenue from the late 1840s, an expansion which reflects the growth of the suburb. There were confectioners, chandlers, boot-makers, tailors, drapers, milliners, dairies, bakers and vintners.

Today, some businesses still retain the atmosphere of the old days – Donovan's Traditional Family Butchers are second-generation craft butchers and have been in Rathgar for over forty years. They have won many awards, including the All-Ireland White Pudding Competition. John Byrne and Sons, Family Butchers has been trading for nearly 100 years, as has the Gourmet Shop across the road, which, despite its modern-sounding name, is a long-established business.

FROM THE VINTRY TO COMANS

The Vintry, with its ornate clock over the entrance, has earned its status as an award-winning off-licence. The clock itself is interesting in that it has a vine encircling its face and a bunch of grapes at its base. The stained-glass doorway also bears symbols of the wine business. The Vintry is a most charming shop that retains a classically old-world feel. The distressed shelving and exposed wooden flooring reinforce this impression. The owners and staff are passionate about wine and they have received awards to prove it. The other side of their business is education. They run wine appreciation courses and have a wine club, both of which take place in a tasting room upstairs. Moreover, they are very much involved in the annual Bloomsday celebrations in Rathgar.

The Rathgar Bookshop, an independent bookstore, is next door and really adds to the village feel of the area. Its book launches and book evenings, as well as its relaxed and inviting atmosphere, suggest that this is what a bookshop should be about.

MacDonald Cycles, around the corner from the ever-popular Bijou restaurant and delicatessen, has been mending bikes since 1922 when the family business opened on Bride Street in Dublin's Liberties. The Rathgar branch opened in 1993. The old Piano Shop is no more, nor is Frizzante's boutique, where, they used to say, 'there is always something new'. Stephanie Parisot's portrait photographer studio and window continue to add colour, atmosphere and imagination to the village. And if you desire to temporarily leave the pleasant confines of the area, Rathgar Travel, in business since 1982, will gladly help you on your way.

There was no bank in Rathgar until the Munster & Leinster Bank opened in 1910, next door to Comans pub. In 1947 it transferred business to the present AIB site just across the road, after Victoria Lodge was demolished. Comans expanded into the bank's former premises and has latterly been the home of the pub's bar, now called Bottler's Bank as a gesture to the bank that once occupied the building. The area where the bathrooms are located today used to be the bank's old vault.

The name Munster & Leinster is still carved on the outer wall. The site on which Comans sits was once the local grocery, which had a small pub at the front of it. There was also an old well on the site, so it was an appropriate place for a tavern. The well is still in use, particularly at times of water shortages.

The year 1847 is inscribed in large lettering on the wall of Comans. At the opposite corner of Rathgar Avenue, 1851 used to be inscribed (before recent demolition) on the 108 pub, suggesting that taverns were located on these corners since the mid-nineteenth century. The name Comans has been on the 1847 premises since the Coman family established themselves in the public house in early 1958. Still a family-run lounge and bar, Comans is very much at the heart of Rathgar. The family began by bottling their own Guinness stout and soon became the bottling suppliers for the local pubs. This has grown into the well-known Comans Wholesale, which services pubs and clubs across Dublin. There is an interesting old picture in the atmospheric Bottler's Bank bar with the name P. Coman over a grocer's and spirit dealer's in Cashel in the nineteenth century. The family can trace its involvement in the licensed trade back to County Tipperary in the early 1800s.

THE GOURMET SHOP – A RATHGAR TREASURE

Located at 48 Highfield Road, the Gourmet Shop premises have been a grocer's since the 1870s. It changed hands several times before Leverett & Frye, who specialised in gourmet food, took over in 1905. Leverett & Frye's was the first shop to import avocados. When they closed in 1968 it became the Gourmet Shop, which still delights with its enticing windows and interior. It is a veritable Aladdin's cave, full of culinary treasures.

It was from the Leverett & Frye famous grocery chain that brothers Seán and Tommy Cronin learnt their trade, both working in the Grafton Street and Dundrum branches before setting up the family-run business that continues thriving to this day in Rathgar. Nowadays, despite the disappearance of many traditional, independent shops, the Gourmet Shop still retains a local, unique and personal feel.

The burgundy-painted exterior and the antique-style lettering on the shop sign make you feel as though you are in another time. This impression is enhanced by the authentic interior, where exclusive, high-quality goods and top-class wines are displayed. There is an excellent choice of cheeses and various cuts of cold meats available.

It is a shop for food aficionados. People travel from all over the country to come to this shop especially at Christmas to buy quality dried fruit for Christmas cakes. Many customers say it isn't Christmas until they enter the Gourmet Shop. Christmas hampers from the shop are a hugely popular gift.

One frequent customer described it as 'nothing short of an Aladdin's cave, full of culinary treasures'. She continued: 'Where else in Dublin can you buy a single nutmeg or cinnamon stick while shopping for eggs, marmalade oranges, homemade coleslaw, a perfect Wicklow cheese, a six-pack of refreshing Limonata, a bottle of best malt or Blandy's Madeira, organic grains, Gentleman's Relish, pickled walnuts, great chocolate and custom-made hampers? I don't think there's anywhere quite like it left in Ireland. Long may it flourish.'[139]

Seán Cronin, the owner of the Gourmet Shop, noted that in the early days some customers would ring in their orders and then collect them later or some even send their drivers. Many interesting and well-known people have patronised the shop, including Abbey actress Siobhán McKenna and her husband Denis O'Dea. Douglas Gageby of *The Irish Times* was a frequent visitor. He never tired of talking about his passion for oak trees. Some, like Lady Ross, lived further afield and sent her chauffeur to collect her order. Sir Anthony de Hoghton (he always stipulated Hoghton without the 'u') was larger than life. On one occasion he hired his usual taxi driver to take him to Germany for a dental appointment. He enjoyed having the Gourmet caviar for breakfast at the counter of the shop.

No list of visitors to the Gourmet Shop would be complete without mentioning Michael. Many of the older residents of Rathgar remember Michael, who frequently stopped customers on their way in to sing them a song and kiss ladies' hands![140]

MEMORIES OF OLD RATHGAR

The Cronins also noted the many changes in the village over the years. There was a long roll call of shops and their owners, most of whom are gone. Miss Doris Orr ran a fruit-and-vegetable shop across the road from the Gourmet. Close to her, Mr Davis had his well-known newsagents which later became Rathgar post office. Then there was Fogarty's grocery shop. Mr Kershaw had a pork butcher beyond Comans. Shortly before Christmas one year, his shop was raided and all his hams and butcher's knives were stolen. On that side of the road also were the Deveneys. They had a grocery shop and off-licence. Nearby was Callally's electrical shop. Close by to the Gourmet, Paddy Quigley had a hardware shop, which was well known amongst DIY enthusiasts and builders in and around the village. Beyond the Gourmet, just on Highfield Road, were car showrooms run by Mr Brochelbank. Around the corner from the Gourmet, Hayes Conyngham had a branch of their chemist shops and Mr Gardiner ran his chemist shop just across the road. Next door to Gardiner's was Mrs Bodkin's Kiddicraft. She was succeeded in the business by her son. Down the road were the Clancy brothers – Kevin, Dominick and

Gerry – who ran a grocery shop for many years. Penelope's Cake Shop, run by the Sheridan family, was a well-known landmark and Keeley's, where the Organic Supermarket is now located, was owned and run by Mrs Horton. It was where everyone went for their stationery and their children's toys. George's Garage will be well remembered.[141]

BIBLIOGRAPHY

Ball, Francis Erlington, *A History of the County Dublin* Part 11 (Dublin: Alex Thom, 1903).

Barry, Michael, *Victorian Dublin Revealed* (Dublin: Andalus Press, 2011).

Bennet, D., *Encyclopedia of Dublin* (Dublin: Gill & MacMillan, 1991).

Corcoran, Michael, *Through Streets Broad and Narrow: A History of Dublin Trams* (Laois: Midland Publishing, 2000).

Costello, Peter, *Dublin Churches* (Dublin: Gill & MacMillan, 1989).

Costello, Peter, *James Joyce: The Years of Growth 1992–1915: A Biography* (London: Kyle Cathie, 1992).

Curtis, Maurice, *Challenge to Democracy: Militant Catholic in Modern Ireland* (Dublin: The History Press Ireland, 2010).

Curtis, Maurice, *Glasnevin* (Dublin: The History Press Ireland, 2013).

Curtis, Maurice, *Portobello* (Dublin: The History Press Ireland, 2012).

Curtis, Maurice, *Rathfarnham* (Dublin: The History Press Ireland, 2014).

Curtis, Maurice, *Rathmines* (Dublin: The History Press Ireland, 2011).

Curtis, Maurice, *The Liberties* (Dublin: The History Press Ireland, 2013).

Curtis, Maurice, *To Hell or Monto: Dublin's Most Notorious Districts* (Dublin: The History Press Ireland, 2015).

D'Alton, John, *The History of County Dublin* (Dublin: Hodges & Smith, 1838).

Daly, Mary E., *Dublin: The Deposed Capital: A Social and Economic History 1960–1914* (Cork: Cork University Press, 1984).

Daly, Mary, Mona Hearn and Peter Pearson, *Dublin Victorian Houses* (Dublin: A&A Farmar,1998).

Dixon, Fred E., *The History of Rathgar* (Dublin: F.E. Dixon, 1989).

Donnelly, Nicholas, *A Short History of Some Dublin Parishes* Part 6, Section 3 (Dublin: CTSI, 1908).

Dungan, Myles, *If You Want to Know Who We Are: The Rathmines and Rathgar Musical Society 1913–2013* (Dublin: Gill & MacMillan, 2013).

Gilbert, John T., *A History of the City of Dublin* (Reprint of 1854 edition. Dublin: Gill & MacMillan, 1978).

Joyce, Weston St John, *The Neighbourhood of Dublin* (Dublin: Gill & Sons, 1912 and 1939).

Kelly, Deirdre, *Four Roads to Dublin* (Dublin: O'Brien Press, 2001).

McManus, Ruth, *Dublin 1910–1940: Shaping the City and Suburbs* (Dublin: Four Courts Press, 2002).

MacNamara, Angela, *Yours Sincerely* (Dublin: Veritas, 1999).

O'Connell, Angela, *The Rathmines Township: A Chronology and Guide to Sources of Information* (Dublin: Angela O'Connell, 1998).

O'Connell, Angela, *The Servants' Church: A History of the Church of the Three Patrons in the Parish of Rathgar* (Dublin: PDR/Church of the Three Patrons, 2004).

Ó Maitiú, Séamas, *Rathmines Township 1847–1930* (Dublin: Séamas Ó Maitiú, 1997).

Ó Maitiú, Séamas, *Dublin's Suburban Towns 1834–1930* (Dublin: Four Courts Press, 2003).

Pearson, Peter, *Decorative Dublin* (Dublin: O'Brien Press, 2002).

Redmond, Reggie, *The History of Oakland Rathgar* (Dublin: St Luke's Hospital, 2008).

Somervile-Large, Peter, *Dublin* (London: Hamish Hamilton, 1979).

Williams, Jeremy, *Architecture in Ireland, 1837–1921: A Companion Guide* (Dublin: Irish Academic Press, 1994).

NOTES

1   Nicholas Donnelly, *A Short History of Some Dublin Parishes*, Part 3, Section 6 (Dublin: CTSI, 1908), p.104; Weston St John Joyce, *The Neighbourhood of Dublin* (Dublin: Gill & Sons, 1912 and 1939), pp.171–4; Ball, Francis Erlington, *A History of the County Dublin* Part 11 (Dublin: Alex Thom, 1903), pp.144–6.

2   Francis Erlington Ball, *A History of the County Dublin* Part 11 (Dublin: Alex Thom, 1903), pp.144–7; Maurice Curtis, *Rathmines* (Dublin: The History Press Ireland, 2011), pp.26–9.

3   Nicholas Donnelly, *A Short History of Some Dublin Parishes* Part 3, Section 6 (Dublin: CTSI, 1908), p.104–7.

4   John Dalton, *The History of County Dublin* (Dublin: Hodges & Smith, 1838), pp.392–3.

5   Nicholas Donnelly, *A Short History of Some Dublin Parishes* Part 3, Section 6 (Dublin: CTSI, 1908), p.104; Weston St John Joyce, *The Neighbourhood of Dublin* (Dublin: Gill & Sons, 1912 and 1939), pp.171–4; Francis Erlington Ball, *History of the County Dublin* (Dublin: Alex Thom, 1903), pp.144–6.

6   Reggie Redmond, *The History of Oakland Rathgar* (Dublin: St Luke's Hospital, 2008), pp.3–5.

7   *Freeman's Journal*, 17 March 1798.

8   *Freeman's Journal*, 1 November 1798.

9   Reggie Redmond, *The History of Oakland Rathgar* (Dublin: St Luke's Hospital, 2008), pp.14–15.

10 Ibid., p.20.

11 *Motor News*, 18 May 1902; Reggie Redmond, *The History of Oakland Rathgar* (2008), pp.23–4.

12 Reggie Redmond. *The History of Oakland Rathgar*. (Dublin: St.Luke's Hospital, 2008). p.26.

13 *Taylor's Map 1816*.

14 Samuel Lewis, *A Topographical Dictionary of Ireland* (London: S. Lewis,1837), p.210.

15 Mary Daly and Mona Hearn, *Dublin Victorian Houses* (Dublin: A&A Farmar,1998), pp.3–8; Séamus Ó Maitiú, *Dublin's Suburban Towns 1834–1930*

(Dublin: Four Courts Press, 2003), pp.63–66; Maurice Curtis, *To Hell or Monto* (Dublin: The History Press Ireland, 2015).

16 Nicholas Donnelly, *A Short History of Some Dublin Parishes* (1908), p.105.

17 Mary Daly and Mona Hearn, *Dublin Victorian Houses* (Dublin: A&A Farmar, 1998), p.35; Maurice Curtis, *Rathmines* (Dublin: The History Press Ireland, 2011), pp.66–73.

18 Mary Daly and Mona Hearn, *Dublin Victorian Houses* (Dublin: A&A Farmar, 1998), p.8–11; Maurice Curtis, *Rathmines* (Dublin: The History Press Ireland, 2011), pp.66–73.

19 Maurice Curtis, *Rathmines* (Dublin: The History Press Ireland, 2011), pp.66–73; Séamas Ó Maitiú, *Dublin's Suburban Towns 1834–1930* (Dublin: Four Courts Press, 2003), pp.63–66.

20 Angela O'Connell, *Rathmines Township 1847–1930* (Dublin: Angela O'Connell, 1997); Séamas Ó Maitiú, *Dublin's Suburban Towns 1834–1930* (Dublin: Four Courts Press, 2003), pp.63–66.

21 Séamus Ó Maitiú, *Dublin's Suburban Towns 1834–1930* (Dublin: Four Courts Press, 2003), pp.63–66.

22 Angela O'Connell, *Rathmines Township 1847–1930* (Dublin: Angela O'Connell, 1997); Séamas Ó Maitiú, *Dublin's Suburban Towns 1834–1930* (Dublin: Four Courts Press, 2003), pp.63–66.

23 Denis Hilliard and Percy Browne, *Zion Church Rathgar 1861–1986* (Dublin: Zion Church Rathgar, 1986), p.7.

24 Mary Daly and Mona Hearn, *Dublin's Victorian Houses* (Dublin: A&A Farmar, 1998), p.39; Michael Barry, *Victorian Dublin Revealed* (Dublin: Andalus Press, 2011), p.61.

25 Mary Daly and Mona Hearn, *Dublin's Victorian Houses* (Dublin: A&A Farmar, 1998), p.128; Michael Barry, *Victorian Dublin Revealed* (Dublin: Andalus Press, 2011), p.61.

26 Angela O'Connell, *The Servants' Church: A History of the Church of Three Patrons Rathgar* (Dublin: PDR/Church of the Three Patrons, 2004), pp.8–9; Mary Daly and Mona Hearn, *Dublin's Victorian Houses* (Dublin: A&A Farmar, 1998), pp.83–86; Michael Barry, *Victorian Dublin Revealed* (Dublin: Andalus Press, 2011), p. 61; Mary Daly, Mona Hearn, *Dublin's Victorian Houses* (Dublin: A&A Farmar, 1998), p.128; Michael Barry, *Victorian Dublin Revealed* (Dublin: Andalus Press, 2011), p.75.

27 Mary Daly and Mona Hearn, *Dublin's Victorian Houses* (Dublin: A&A Farmar, 1998), pp.35–42; Séamus Ó Maitiú, *Dublin's Suburban Towns 1834–1930* (Dublin: Four Courts Press, 2003), pp.63–6; Maurice Curtis, *Rathmines* (Dublin: The History Press Ireland, 2011), pp.66–73.

28 Mary Daly, Mona Hearn and Peter Pearson, *Dublin Victorian Houses* (Dublin: A&A Farmar, 1998), p.128; Michael Corcoran, *Through Streets Broad and Narrow: A History of Dublin Trams* (Laois: Midland Publishing, 2000); Michael Barry, *Victorian Dublin Revealed* (Dublin: Andalus Press, 2011), pp.61, 160.

29 Fred E. Dixon, *The History of Rathgar* (Dublin: F.E. Dixon, 1989), p.8.

30   Mary Daly, Mona Hearn and Peter Pearson, *Dublin Victorian Houses* (Dublin: A&A Farmar, 1998), p.19.

31   Ibid., pp.19–21.

32   Michael Corcoran, *Through Streets Broad and Narrow: A History of Dublin Trams* (Laois: Midland Publishing, 2000).

33   Maurice Curtis, *Rathmines* (Dublin: The History Press Ireland, 2011).

34   Mary Daly, Mona Hearn and Peter Pearson, *Dublin Victorian Houses* (Dublin: A&A Farmar, 1998), p.33; 1913 Dublin Lockout exhibition at the National Library of Ireland, 2013.

35   1913 Dublin Lockout exhibition at the National Library of Ireland, 2013.

36   Michael Corcoran, *Through Streets Broad and Narrow: A History of Dublin Trams* (Laois: Midland Publishing, 2000).

37   Séamus Ó Maitiú, *Dublin's Suburban Towns 1834–1930* (Dublin: Four Courts Press, 2003), pp.63–66.

38   Jimmy O'Dea and Harry O'Donovan, c. 1930; Jimmy O'Dea in Henry Boylan, *A Dictionary of Irish Biography* (Colorado: Roberts Rinehart, 1998), p.314; *The Irish Times*, 8 January 1965.

39   Jimmy O'Dea in Henry Boylan, *A Dictionary of Irish Biography* (Colorado: Roberts Rinehart, 1998), p.314.

40   Angela MacNamara, *Yours Sincerely* (Dublin: Veritas, 1999), p.6.

41   Ibid., p.8.

42   Ibid., p.11.

43   Harold G. Leask, *Christ Church Rathgar: The Story of One Hundred Years* (Dublin: Christ Church Rathgar, 2009), pp.4–8; Peter Costello, *Dublin Churches* (Dublin: Gill & MacMillan, 1989), p.140.

44   Ibid., pp.12–19.

45   Angela O'Connell, *The Servants' Church: A History of the Church of the Three Patrons in the Parish of Rathgar* (Dublin: PDR/Church of the Three Patrons, 2004), pp.11–23; Nicholas Donnelly, *A Short History of Some Dublin Parishes* Part 6, Section 3 (Dublin: CTSI, 1908), pp.103–11.

46   Nicholas Donnelly, *A Short History of Some Dublin Parishes* Part 6, Section 3 (Dublin: CTSI, 1908), pp.105–6; Peter Costello, *Dublin Churches* (Dublin: Gill & MacMillan, 1989), p.140.

47   *The Irish Times*, 20 March 1860.

48   Jeremy Williams, *Architecture in Ireland, 1837–1921: A Companion Guide* (Dublin: Irish Academic Press, 1994), p.187.

49   John Brennan, 'Thomas MacDonagh. A Personal Memoir'; *The Irish Times*, 3 May 2015.

50   Denis Hilliard and Percy Brown, *Zion Church Rathgar: A Brief Account of its History 1861–1986* (Dublin: Zion Church, 1986), pp.7–8.

51   *Irish Builder*, 2 July 1859.

52   Patrick Comerford blog, 31 December 2013; information from Grosvenor Road Baptist church.

53   Peter Costello, *Dublin Churches* (Dublin: Gill & MacMillan, 1989), p.138; information from Brighton Road Methodist church.

54 Fred E. Dixon, *The History of Rathgar* (Dublin: F.E. Dixon, 1989), pp.12–15;
    Peter Pearson, *Decorative Dublin* (Dublin: O'Brien Press, 2002), p.120.

55 Michael Corcoran, *Through Streets Broad and Narrow: A History of Dublin
    Trams* (Laois: Midland Publishing, 2000), p.128; Michael Barry, *Victorian
    Dublin Revealed* (Dublin: Andalus Press, 2011), p.61.

56 Turtle Bunbury website; interview with Donnacha O'Dea, Olympic swimmer
    and poker player, N.D.

57 Ibid.

58 *Bureau of Military History: Statement of Witness Colonel Eamon Broy. Document
    No. W.S. 1284;* obituary in *The Irish Press,* 24 January 1972.

59 Obituary in *Inniú,* 30 December 1955.

60 Nicholas Donnelly, *A Short History of Some Dublin Parishes* Part 6, Section 3
    (Dublin: CTSI, 1908) p.104.

61 Michael Barry, *Victorian Dublin Revealed* (Dublin: Andalus Press, 2011), p.52.

62 David Kerr, *A History of Rathgar National School 1908–1996* (Dublin: Rathgar
    National Schools, 1996), pp.6–8.

63 Ibid. p.4; Michael Barry, *Victorian Dublin Revealed* (Dublin: Andalus Press,
    2011), p.109.

64 David Kerr, *A History of Rathgar National School 1908–1996* (Dublin: Rathgar
    National Schools, 1996), pp.16–19, 32–3.

65 Nicholas Allan, *George Russell (Æ) and the New Ireland 1905–3* (Dublin: Four
    Courts Press, 2003), pp.4–9.

66 Henry Boylan, *A Dictionary of Irish Biography* (Colorado: Roberts Rinehart,
    1994), p.384.

67 *The Irish Times,* 18 June 2015.

68 Jeremy Williams, *Architecture in Ireland, 1837–1921: A Companion Guide* (Dublin:
    Irish Academic Press,1994), p.188.

69 Maurice Curtis, *Rathmines* (Dublin: The History Press Ireland, 2011).

70 Transcript of evidence of Julia O'Donovan, 10 Garville Avenue, Rathgar,
    in files of the Bureau of Military History, 15 February 1951. Ref. No. W.S.475.

71 'Charles Lynch – An Appreciation', *The Irish Times,* 24 September 1984; Hal
    O'Brien of Airfield Road.

72 George Barnett Smith, 'Carleton, William 1794–1869' in *Dictionary of
    National Biography* (London: Smith, Elder and Co., 1899), p.234.

73 Weston St John Joyce, *The Neighbourhood of Dublin* (Dublin: Gill & Sons, 1912
    and 1939), pp.171–4; Peter Pearson, *Decorative Dublin* (Dublin: O'Brien Press,
    2002), pp.26, 68, 76, 78, 114, 120.

74 Michael Barry, *Victorian Dublin Revealed* (Dublin: Andalus Press, 2011), pp.52–6,
    95–6.

75 Mary Daly, Mona Hearn and Peter Pearson, *Dublin Victorian Houses* (Dublin:
    A&A Farmar, 1998), pp.135–7.

76 Ibid.; Fred E. Dixon, *The History of Rathgar* (Dublin: F.E. Dixon, 1989), pp.3–9.

77 Michael Barry, *Victorian Dublin Revealed* (Dublin: Andalus Press, 2011),
    pp.52–56; 95–96.

78 Ibid., pp.52–6, 95–6; Mary Daly, Mona Hearn and Peter Pearson, *Dublin*

Victorian Houses (Dublin: A&A Farmar, 1998), pp.133–54.

79 Michael Barry, *Victorian Dublin Revealed* (Dublin: Andalus Press, 2011), pp.52–6; 95–6; Fred E. Dixon. *The History of Rathgar*. (Dublin: F.E. Dixon, 1989), p.7.

80 Peter Pearson, *Decorative Dublin* (Dublin: O'Brien Press, 2002), pp.112–15. Mary Daly, Mona Hearn and Peter Pearson *Dublin Victorian Houses* (Dublin: A&A Farmar, 1998); Michael Barry, *Victorian Dublin Revealed* (Dublin: Andalus Press, 2011), 95–6.

81 Fred E. Dixon, *The History of Rathgar* (Dublin: F.E. Dixon, 1989), p.11.

82 Niamh Whitfield 'Order Cancelling the 1916 Rising', *The Irish Times*, 17 March 2014.

83 Dublin Civic Museum.

84 Thanks to Michael McGarry of Frankfurt Avenue.

85 Fred E. Dixon, *The History of Rathgar* (Dublin: F.E. Dixon, 1989), pp.20–3.

86 Jeremy Williams, *Architecture in Ireland, 1837–1921: A Companion Guide* (Dublin: Irish Academic Press, 1994), p.188.

87 Ibid.

88 *The Irish Times*, 26 January 1935 (Report on the Inquest); Mark Keenan on Clarendon in the *rish Independent*, 2 February 2015.

89 Weston St John Joyce, *The Neighbourhood of Dublin* (Dublin; Gill & Sons, 1912 and 1939), p.171; Peter Pearson, *Decorative Dublin* (2002), pp.76–7.

90 Fred E. Dixon, *The History of Rathgar* (Dublin: F.E. Dixon, 1989), p.12.

91 Thanks to the Irish Georgian Society and the Lucena Clinic, Orwell Road.

92 Thanks to the Redemptorist Community, Marianella, Orwell Road; Interview 15 July 2015 with Laetetia Lefroy, whose family owned Faunagh House.

93 Michael Barry, *Victorian Dublin Revealed* (Dublin: Andalus Press, 2011), p.53.

94 *Dictionary of Irish Architects 1720–1940* (Dublin: Irish Architectural Archive, 2015); E.M. Cosgrave. *Dublin and County Dublin in the Twentieth Century* (Brighton: W.T. Pike, 1908), p.264.

95 Niall Meehan, 'Church and State and the Bethany Home', *History Ireland*, Vol.18, No.5, pp.5–8.

96 Ibid.

97 Martin Joyce talk given to the Rathgar Residents' Association; Christopher Moriarty. *Down the Dodder* (Dublin: Wolfhound Press, 1998), p.25.

98 Caoimhe Fox, *Newsfour* June/July 2015; Christopher Moriarty, *Down the Dodder* (Dublin: Wolfhound Press, 1998), pp.25, 11; *The Irish Press*, 4 July 1933, p.3.

99 Caoimhe Fox, *Newsfour*, June/July 2015; Christopher Moriarty, *Down the Dodder* (Dublin: Wolfhound Press, 1998), pp.25, 11; *The Irish Press*, 4 July 1933, p.3.

100 Maurice Curtis, *Rathmines* (Dublin: The History Press Ireland, 2011).

101 Mary Daly, Mona Hearn and Peter Pearson, *Dublin Victorian Houses* (Dublin: A&A Farmar, 1998), p.17.

102 Ibid., pp.53–5.

103 Peter Pearson, *Decorative Dublin* (Dublin: O'Brien Press, 2002), p.26.

104 Maurice Curtis, *Rathfarnham* (Dublin: The History Press Ireland, 2013).

105 Libby McElroy of Trinity Hall.

106 Hugh Oram, 'An Irishman's Diary', *The Irish Times*, 30 June 2015; Michael MacCann, gardener at the Trinity College Dublin's Botanic Garden in Dartry.

107 Maurice Curtis, *Rathmines* (Dublin: The History Press Ireland, 2011).

108 Obituary in the *Irish Independent*, 29 June 1995.

109 Jeremy Williams, *Architecture in Ireland, 1837–1921: A Companion Guide* (Dublin: Irish Academic Press, 1994), p.190.

110 Stratford College, 2015.

111 Bewley's Café of Grafton Street, Dublin, January 2015.

112 Mark O'Brien, *The Irish Times: A History* (2008), pp.186–90; 268–9; *BBC News*, 20 July 2011.

113 Jim Ring. 'Childers, Robert Erskine 1870–1922' in *The Oxford Dictionary of National Biography* (Oxford, OUP, 2004).

114 Arnold Bax, *Farewell My Youth* (Scolar Press, reprint edition, 1992), p.29.

115 Séamas de Barra, 'Into the Twilight: Arnold Bax and Ireland, *The Journal of Music in Ireland*, March/April 2004, pp.25–9.

116 Jeremy Williams, *Architecture in Ireland, 1837–1921: A Companion Guide* (Dublin: Irish Academic Press, 1994), p.190.

117 Ibid.

118 Michael Barry, *Victorian Dublin Revealed* (Dublin:Andalus Press, 2011), p.54–55; Mary Daly, Mona Hearn and Peter Pearson, *Dublin Victorian Houses*. (Dublin: A&A Farmar, 1998), p.30.

119 Elizabeth Birdthistle in *The Irish Times*, 14 May 2015.

120 Jeremy Williams. *Architecture of Ireland 1837–1921: A Companion Guide*, (Dublin: Irish Academic Press, 1994), p.190.

121 Ibid.

122 Maurice Curtis, *Rathmines* (Dublin: The History Press Ireland, 2011).

123 Eason's bookshop, O'Connell Street, Dublin; Mary Daly, Mona Hearn and Peter Pearson, *Dublin Victorian Houses* (Dublin: A&A Farmar, 1998), p.10; Maurice Curtis, *Challenge to Democracy: Militant Catholicism in Modern Ireland* (Dublin: The History Press Ireland, 2010), pp.81-91.

124 Maurice Curtis, *Challenge to Democracy: Militant Catholicism in Modern Ireland* (Dublin: The History Press Ireland, 2010), pp.81–91.

125 Kevin McDermott, 'Obituary to Peggy Jordan' in *Rambling House* (2000)

126 *The Irish Times*, 30 July 2005.

127 Personal reminiscences and thanks to the Opperman family.

128 Mary Daly, Mona Hearn and Peter Pearson. *Dublin Victorian Houses* (Dublin: A&A Farmar, 1998), p.24.

129 *Irish Independent*, 20 May 2004.

130 James Joyce Centre, Dublin; Peter Costello, *James Joyce: The Years of Growth 1882–1915: A Biography* (London: Kyle Cathie, 1992), pp.57–9.

131 Peter Costello, *James Joyce: The Years of Growth 1882–1915: A Biography* (London: Kyle Cathie, 1992), pp.57–9.

132 Ibid.

133 David Robbins, *The Irish Independent*, 20 May 2004; Peter Costello, *James*

Joyce: The Years of Growth 1882–1915: A Biography (London: Kyle Cathie,1992), pp.57–9.

134 Ashbrook Tennis Club, 2015.

135 Maurice Curtis, *Rathmines* (Dublin: The History Press Ireland, 2011).

136 Rathmines and Rathgar Musical Society, 2015; Myles Dungan, *If You Want to Know Who We Are: The Rathmines and Rathgar Musical Society 1913–2013* (Dublin: Gill & MacMillan, 2013).

137 Ibid.

138 Weston St John Joyce, *The Neighbourhood of Dublin* (Dublin: Gill & Sons, 1912 and 1939), pp.169–73.

139 Reminiscences of Helen Rock; Marion Fitzgerald, 'Memories of Selling Caviar by the Kilo', *The Irish Times*, 15 June 1985.

140 Ibid.; Thanks to Seán Cronin of the Gourmet Shop.

141 Reminiscences of Seán and Tommy Cronin, the Gourmet Shop, Rathgar.

Also from The History Press

IRELAND
AT WAR